The Art of Tent Camping

By Russ Steffy
And
Steve White, Technical Advisor

NOTICE

Information in this document is subject to change without notice. Companies, names, and data used in examples herein are fictitious unless otherwise noted. No part of this document may be reproduced or transmitted in any form or by any means, electronic or mechanical, for any purpose, without the express written permission of **THE AUTHOR**. **THE AUTHOR** makes no warranty of any kind with regard to this material, including, but not limited to, the implied warranties of merchantability and fitness for a particular purpose. **THE AUTHOR** shall not be liable for errors contained herein or for incidental or consequential damages in connection with the furnishing, performance, or use of this material.

© 2011 - 2014

SECOND EDITION

ISBN-10: 1478330023
ISBN-13: 978-1478330028

Buck is a registered trademark of Buck Knives.

Coleman is a registered trademark of The Coleman Company, Inc.

MagLite is a registered trademark of Mag Instrument, Inc.

About This Guide

The Art of Tent Camping is a guide designed for the casual camper wishing to explore our mountains and deserts taking nothing more than what can be packed into and on a conventional vehicle. The goal is simplicity, relative ease, and most of all, comfort while enjoying the outdoors. The highest priority next to safety when taking family and friends on a camping trip is *comfort*. This may mean more gear in more vehicles, but a little bit of planning ahead and the right equipment will result in a successful outing.

The Art of Tent Camping includes a comprehensive list of equipment, however, that doesn't mean you have to take all of the equipment on every outing. The season in which your trip is planned, the type of camping you'll be doing, and the location suggests the appropriate equipment to take along. And even if you're not taking the whole family, *The Art of Tent Camping* describes techniques for "downsizing" - you don't need a moving van to camp comfortably!

Emergency preparedness is a vital practice which must be constantly addressed and maintained. As you read this guide, you'll see it has also been designed to serve as "double duty" in the event of an emergency at home. The resources you spend on camping equipment, provisions, and preparation is working much harder than you might have thought and could potentially save lives.

Acknowledgments

To my wife Gloria, a real trooper who tolerates my enthusiasm for our outdoor treks, and won't leave home without her iron.

To my daughter Laura, who I am absolutely sure will never, ever, become a herpetologist.

To Leslie, Emily, and Anthony, the rest of my troops who always pitch in without my having to ask.

And, to my good friend Steve, a very analytical, no nonsense guy, posed perhaps the most challenging philosophical question I have ever encountered: "In two sentences or less, give me a definition of 'Common Sense'". To which I replied after pondering for quite some time, "Never look up with your mouth open".

About the Author

I possess over forty years of camping experience in a variety of environments. But let me be clear about what I am not; I do not claim to be a mountaineer, rock climber, or survivalist. I am not one of those guys on those extreme survival shows, nor do I care to be. However, I do pay close attention to preparedness for any emergency I may have to engage. It may be of interest to note that I am a network administrator by profession which may account for my passion of spending so much time in the outdoors. A passion which also allows me to completely shed myself of all things technical, and even more importantly for me, take a break from the general population. One of the secrets to a successful camping trip is to get as far away from the vast majority of civilization in as little time as possible without having to spend days traveling to and from your destination.

My first serious experiences with the outdoors began when I followed in the footsteps of my older brother and joined the Boy Scouts in the late 1960's. Our troop was extremely active, at least one camping trip per month, all of which included a hike in and out of the campsite wearing a full pack. Back in those days parents would drop their kids off for a weekend camping trip with Army style packs including blankets (no sleeping bags, no sleeping pads, lucky if they thought of a poncho), a cast iron skillet or two, a pair of loafers (no hiking boots), and nothing that could pass for a tent. Somehow, I ended up becoming a Patrol Leader and spent most of my scouting time mentoring new scouts (and parents), for obvious reasons.

I might add that very serious emphasis was placed on the Scouts back then by educating them in all areas of survival, including building emergency shelters, fire starting, field cooking, emergency first aid, edible plants, poisonous plants, snakes, and insects, to name a few. One must realize the United States was fighting a particularly brutal war at the time, and although we had no idea, we were being prepared for possible participation in that conflict.

As a young adult I continued to take trips into the High Sierra of California and other parts of Northern California, many of which lasted a week or more. While I have never attempted such adventures during the height of winter, I can tell you even in the warmest months I have backpacked through spectacular electrical storms, hurricane force winds, and ping-pong ball sized hail. I have spent many a night camped well above the tree line (tree line being about 9,000 feet) where the night skies are crystal clear, and even without the moon a flashlight is not necessary because star light offers more than enough luminance to see.

Ah but inevitably, marriage followed by child briefly interrupted my periodic adventures into the great outdoors. My daughter was three when I took her and mom on her first camping trip. It was a weekend trip with everything we needed packed into and on top of our sedan. Our immediate family continued to grow with the addition of nieces and nephews, all of whom I have taken on various adventures. Thus began another chapter in my camping experience which I am sharing with you in this guide.

About our Technical Advisor

Mr. White is mechanical engineer by profession and shares my passion for camping. Mr. White's contributions to this guide are numerous, from equipment modifications, tips on dealing with insects, to most of the section devoted to basic fishing techniques. Mr. White is an expert craftsman with a broad working knowledge of various tools and materials and whose professional experience and near-perfect understanding of common sense, made this guide possible.

Table of Contents

Chapter 1 Let's Get Started

Depending on just how casual of a camping trip you are interested in will determine the level of quality of the equipment you will need. Obviously, if you plan to spend a week in the Alaskan Tundra, you will need shelter rated to withstand gale force winds and sleeping bags for sub-zero temperatures. However, for the purposes of this guide I am going to assume we are not on a research expedition out of McMurdo Station, but want to actually enjoy camping. So I am going to base my suggested equipment and provision requirements on the following criteria:

1) Temperatures ranging from 40 degrees to 105 degrees Fahrenheit.
2) 0 to 20 mph wind with maximum 35 mph gusts.
3) Always plan for a possibility of rain or snow regardless of the season or your planned destination.
4) Always check weather forecasts right up to the last minute. You must always keep in the back of your mind potential threats such as flash floods and forest fires.
5) Length of stay of one to six nights.

While my vehicle is a pickup truck and more suitable for taking a whole family, SUV's and sedans will just as easily accommodate comfortable camping. Much of what I recommend about techniques and equipment can be downsized to accommodate an SUV or sedan. I know, because I've done it. One point worth mentioning here, car top carrier hardware can be expensive, but I recommend investing in the best. If you have an SUV equipped with roof racks, there are plenty of roof top cargo container options to choose from.

Plan Ahead

For a week long trip with family and friends, I begin stocking up on supplies a month or more in advance. One section of my garage is reserved exclusively for camping equipment and provisions. I have a cabinet made of heavy plastic and several heavy duty plastic tubs which stack, (I will go into more detail on this later) and I can pre-pack in advance. The objective is to prepare over time, don't wait until the night before taking off for a week. Plus, this gives you the opportunity to use coupons and obtain goods when they are on sale. Once I have all of the garage based equipment in order, I can concentrate on perishable food items and other last minute issues. Then, it's just a matter of throwing the cabinet, tubs, and coolers into the back the night before leaving. It's quick, easy, and when you use the checklists at the end of this guide you won't get that "what did I forget" feeling once you're on your way.

Check the Weather, 40% Chance of Rain?

Ever wonder what the weather forecasters mean by a "40% chance" of rain? Will it rain 40% of the time? Will it rain over 40% of the area? If you are checking the forecast the night before departure you may want to take the chance of rain into consideration.

Forecasts issued by the National Weather Service typically include a Probability of precipitation (PoP) declaration which is expressed as the "chance of rain" or "chance of precipitation". The PoP describes the chance of precipitation occurring at any selected location in a given area.

How is PoP calculated? Mathematically, PoP is defined as follows:

PoP = C x A where C is equal to the confidence that precipitation will occur somewhere in the forecast area, and where A is equal to the percent of the area that will receive measureable precipitation, if there is any precipitation at all. Using a 40% chance as an example, if the forecaster expects precipitation to occur at a 100% level of confidence, and expects 40% of a given area receiving measurable rain, then PoP = C x A or "1" times ".4" equaling .4 or 40%.

However, most of the time forecasts are expressed as a combination of degree of confidence and area coverage. If the level of confidence is only 50% that measurable rain will occur over 80% of the area, the PoP is 40%, or PoP = .5 x .8 which equals .4 or 40%. In either event, the correct way to interpret the forecast is: there is a 40% chance that rain will occur at any given point in the area.

Or, in my opinion, a 40% chance of rain means a 100% chance of rain over 40% of a given area. I think my definition is easier to understand, and it errors on the side of being better prepared. Besides, you might as well just use a dart board to predict the weather and be prepared for anything.

Leave Behind a "Flight Plan"

More often than not, this "mandatory requirement" simple task is overlooked or forgotten. It does not matter how many adventurers are in your party or how long your trip is planned for, there is simply no excuse for not leaving an itinerary of your outing with at least one responsible adult at home. The minimum itinerary should include names of everyone in your party, an arrival date, an approximate arrival time at the campsite, and the planned last day of the trip. If the destination points are at different campsites over the course of your trip, that information should be included. Maps (topographic maps are highly recommended) of the area you will be visiting as well as any planned day hikes you will be traveling should be highlighted. Maps should be provided as part of your flight plan. I understand that plans can, and especially when camping, might change. Highlighting the general area on the maps helps solve this problem in the event of an emergency. At least the search and rescue teams have some clue as to where to look for those in need of assistance. Never leave home without filing a flight plan.

Primitive Camping

Primitive camping, as opposed to camping in a developed campground, offers an additional set of challenges. But the pay off typically includes no next door neighbors, unlimited choice of campsites, and no posted rules such as how to park your vehicle and how many vehicles you can park per campsite, and so on.

This doesn't mean there aren't any rules, just fewer rules as one might expect in less densely populated areas. Primitive camping probably means there will be no readily available drinking water. Make sure you take plenty of water and provisions when traveling in undeveloped areas. The primary requirement for primitive camping is *common sense*.

Some years ago, an unfortunate event occurred in Death Valley, California. A mother and her teenage son became stuck up to the axles in soft sand in their four wheel drive vehicle during the month of August. That means daytime temperatures upwards of 125 degrees Fahrenheit (The highest recorded temperature is 136 making Death Valley the hottest place on earth). It was several days before they were found, her son didn't make it. They didn't have nearly enough water to begin with, but they had no business being there at that time of year in the first place. *Common sense* or lack thereof, cost a young life in this case.

The Bureau of Land Management (BLM), under the jurisdiction of the Federal government, oversees vast areas of wilderness with much of it open to the public. There are designated wilderness areas within BLM owned land where camping and travel by vehicle are not permitted. All signage should be carefully reviewed. BLM land is patrolled by Federal officers who can issue citations for violating the law.

Here are a few additional suggestions when driving on BLM land and that of other jurisdictions:

- Stay on designated roadways and trails.

- Use a camping area and fire pit which has already been built.

- All personal hygiene should be performed well away from any water source and any area resembling a camp spot. The accepted distance is two to three hundred feet.

- Pack out all your refuse, there likely aren't going to be any trash bins. In fact, pack out trash left by others. If everyone contributed by taking out a little more trash than they brought, imagine how much nicer your favorite primitive spot would be the next time you visit.

- You will likely be out of cell phone range. I recommend taking a CB (Citizens Band) radio. Other primitive campers and off roaders will also have CB radios both for informal communication, and emergencies. Many state and local law enforcement agencies monitor channel 9 on Citizen's Band in the event someone is broadcasting a distress call.

- Many traffic laws apply to off road travel; especially driving under the influence and the transporting of firearms. If you are caught violating these laws, you will be subject to the same consequences as if you were driving to your local grocery store.

Camping in undeveloped areas often means travel may be hazardous by conventional vehicle. Unless your vehicle is suited for off road travel, I suggest staying on paved or gravel roads. I encourage you to explore undeveloped areas and enjoy the benefits of primitive camping. However, I also encourage those who are less experienced with the outdoors to first sharpen their camping skills in developed campgrounds before going too far off the beaten path.

The Drive

Traveling to and from your destination is probably not the best part of your trip. I always plan departure as early in the morning as possible. Avoiding traffic helps minimize stress for me, and I like to get to my camp spot early so I can set up and still have the better part of an extra day to play. Pillows and coats are kept inside the vehicle because chances are the little campers are going to sleep through some of the drive. I recommend keeping snacks and beverages handy and I let everyone know I am more than willing to take a rest stop whenever necessary.

Since I am usually very familiar with the surrounding countryside wherever we go, I like to discuss topics such as history and geology. I also remind everyone about the rules and other topics covered in this guide. Sometimes I will play a game whereby I announce "the first person to see a purple car gets a quarter"! Or, when I know we're traveling through the desert, hours away from the nearest water, I'll offer a quarter to the first person to spot a boat! Well, I can't just give it away.

One trip took us through a couple of hours of an agricultural area including farms and ranches. "Okay", I said as I was pointing to a field of cotton, "The first one to tell me what they're growing there gets a quarter!" That was too easy, lost another quarter. Then I pointed to another field and exclaimed "The first one to tell me what's growing there gets two quarters!" After driving by the field without a correct answer, I exclaimed: "Nothing!" There was nothing growing in the field as it had been plowed over. I thought that was funny but nobody else was laughing. Oh well, you'd had to have been there I guess.

If possible, I plan a different route home offering different scenery which helps keep the little campers from repeating the all time most asked question "when are we going to be home?" Since I am in no hurry to get home, I like to stop at fruit stands and other unusual roadside vendors. Of course, after an extended period of time dining on camping cuisine, nobody complains about stopping at an excellent Mexican restaurant for a real meal. More importantly, the driver should take every opportunity to rest before continuing the journey home.

You know you've had a successful outing when everyone asks "So, when are going camping again?"

Chapter 2 Equipment

Can Drink Holders

The importance of this piece of equipment warrants its' own small section.

The can drink holders I am referring to are made of compressed foam and allow you to insert the can into the holder. The insulating property of the holder, and the fact your warm hand is not in direct contact with the can keeps the drink cooler, longer. You should be able to buy these for about a buck a piece in the camping section of you favorite big box store.

There are also more exotic insulating holders for bottled drinks, some even with a zipper up the side. These are harder to find though. Interestingly enough, insulated can and bottle holders have a reverse affect when used in cold weather. You may not be concerned about your drink getting warm when it's 40 degrees out (about the temperature of the inside of your refrigerator), but holding a cold can in an ungloved hand probably isn't going to be very comfortable.

9

Chairs

I prefer the collapsible models which sell for around $20.00. If they last a season or two I'm happy. You can spend many times that for a better, more comfortable camp chair, but the last time I did someone left it too close to the campfire after retiring for the night melting most of the plastic. Note the handy collapsible table in the picture above.

Tip: I recommend avoiding collapsible chairs for the little campers. I've seen more than a few little fingers get caught in the moving components. Get inflatable or bean bag chairs for the little ones. They are easy to pack and are much safer.

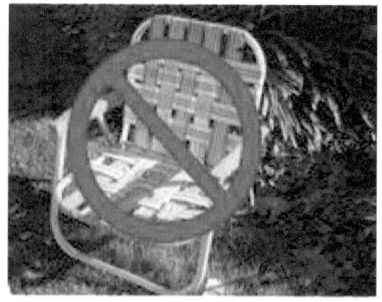

I definitely recommend not buying the cheap folding chairs more commonly used at the beach. They are far less durable, and you have to make sure to tie them down while traveling. Otherwise, they will end up with the rest of the lawn furniture on the side of the roadway.

Clothing

Keep in mind the parameters I defined at the beginning of this guide with regards to temperatures, wind, and always the possibility of rain when considering what clothing and footwear you want to bring on your trip.

The most important piece of clothing is coats. Most likely, the heavy coats you already have are sufficient. I buy coats with a thick lining and always one size larger so I can layer if needed (layering means wearing additional clothing such as a sweatshirt underneath the coat). The coat should be water resistant, and combined with a poncho or rain suit, will get you through spring showers.

Coats designed for colder weather vary in price and purpose. The less expensive designs are comprised of both the filler and lining usually made of 100% Polyester. The more expensive coats are typically lined with Polyester and filled with either duck or goose down (feathers), and the zippers are insulated to help retain body heat. More expensive coats are often sewn together using a "box" type construction. Box construction means there are no seams completely sewn through both the inner and outer lining, again to preserve body heat. Unless you are planning outings outside my suggested comfort criteria, down filled coats are not necessary and actually can get uncomfortably warm.

Serious rain gear, pictured below, is expensive. A decent rain suit can set you back about $100.00. If you invest in a rain suit, I recommend at least one size larger than your heavy coat (which should be one size larger for layering as already mentioned) and pants. The advantage to a rain suit is you can wear seasonal clothing and slip the rain suit on in a minute if you have to. Different rain suits have different ratings for water resistance and breathing, so depending on what you might expect on your camping trips, do a little research.

However, most of the time a heavier gauge vinyl poncho, pictured below, will keep you dry. I prefer ponchos because they also do double duty for covering the firewood and any exposed equipment. Don't buy the cheap thin type, those won't last a single trip.

I've had many experiences in California's Sierra Nevada Mountains and the Northwest where a storm hit in a matter of minutes, even in the warmest months of the year. I always keep ponchos and a couple of tarps within easy reach just in case. I prefer using a sweatshirt and sweatpants in place of long underwear if the weather turns a little chillier than planned. Long underwear has only one practical purpose, a set of sweats can do double-duty. The rest is easy.

For a summer outing, I bring one pair of jeans for the entire trip, and a pair of shorts and tee shirt for every other day of the trip. On all outings I like to bring a clean change of clothes for the trip home. I recommend one bath towel per person for the trip.

Note: Consider wearing wool beanies and socks when sleeping. Most of the body heat is lost through the top of the head and the bottoms of the feet.

Footwear

Footwear should include one sturdy pair of boots or shoes per person suitable for short hiking trips. I recommend flip-flops or sandals for use in camp for comfort, or in case the boots need to dry. I don't like water shoes because they fill up with sediment. If you plan to swim in a lake or river, I suggest an old pair of canvas sneakers, or rubber sandals. Wearing something on the feet in water helps protect against fish hooks and other sharp objects. Gators, pictured below, are lightweight nylon wraps which button at the top and bottom, while the side is secured with Velcro. Gators will offer some protection when walking in light snow or mud assuming your boots are water resistant.

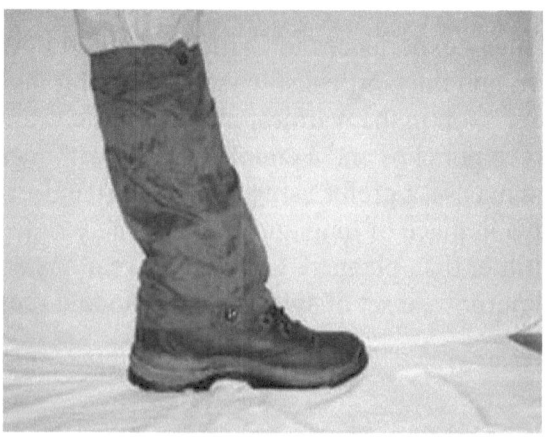

Note: I don't recommend steel toed boots. I have read about cases where a large rock falls on a steel toed boot and nearly severs the wearer's toes.

Tip: I recommend "boot grease" made from bee's wax and bear fat for maintaining and water-proofing leather boots.

Keep Shoes, Sandals, and Boots inside Your Tent

There are several important reasons to store all footwear in your zipped up tent or at least inside your vehicle when not in use. Mainly, you want to avoid leaving shoes and boots outside thereby offering comfortable living quarters for critters such as spiders and scorpions. Footwear, and any other equipment for that matter, left outside unnecessarily exposes your gear to the elements.

I learned the hard way on my first snow camping trip many years ago. I did stow my boots inside the tent for the night. Unfortunately, the temperature dropped to single digits and by morning my boots were frozen solid. Should you ever encounter such extreme conditions, I recommend sleeping with your boots inside your sleeping bag. You don't have to wear them while you're asleep; the idea is to keep them from freezing.

On longer outings, particularly with the kids, I like to take strips of artificial grass to place on the ground at the entrance of each tent. Weigh each corner of the strip with a good sized rock too. And, the strips don't have to be very large, maybe 5 feet by 3 feet. The purpose is to reduce the amount of sand or dirt accumulating inside the tent. It's actually just a door mat for camping.

Get in the habit of always checking shoes and boots before putting them on even if they have been put away. If nothing else, you could be a pawn for an old camping prank – Someone might stuff a raw egg down your boot!

Gloves

Gloves can be just about any type. If it looks like colder weather, ski gloves are recommended. I prefer the gauntlet style, the oversize cuffs slide over the sleeves of my coat. I also use leather athletic gloves, the type with the finger tips cut off allowing better use of my hands for setting up or breaking down equipment while offering some measure of warmth:

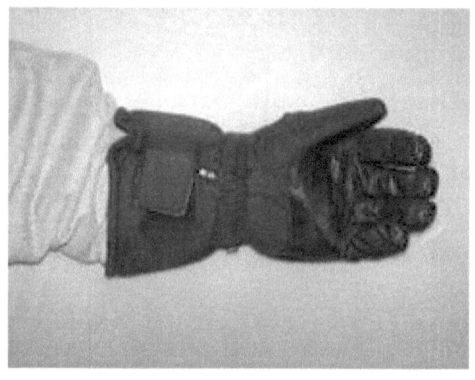

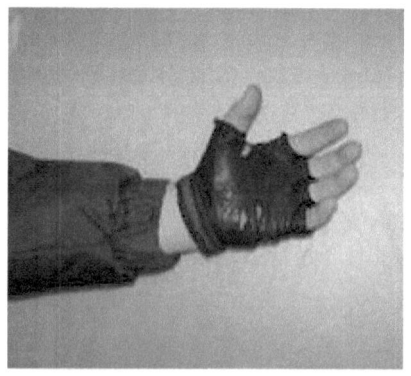

Headgear

During warm weather months, I prefer a wide-brimmed straw hat. They're light, the wider brim offers better protection from the sun, and they vent better which helps keep me cool. I also like canvas headgear because I can soak it in cold water to keep me cool.

Cold weather camping should include wool beanies and hoods on the coats. Otherwise, my preference is for a dark colored ball cap. Dark colors absorb heat from sunlight, while lighter colors reflect sunlight. Use this to your advantage when considering all clothing options for each season of the year.

Cooking Equipment

Assembling a set of cooking equipment for camping may be the easiest task of all. I still have a few aluminum pots with lids from sets I had when I was in the Scouts. I conscripted a couple of no-stick pans from the kitchen exclusively for camping. Pots and pans that are a little too "seasoned" for your kitchen and would otherwise be tossed in the trash are ideal for your camping kitchen. One plastic, and one metal spatula, a large plastic spoon, and you're pretty much set. I also take a small set of flatware for use instead of plastic utensils for environmental purposes, and the fact plastic spoons, forks, and knives won't outlast a day anyway. There is absolutely no need to purchase camping cook sets. Don't waste your money.

Each camper should have their own cup, preferably a metal cup similar to the one pictured below. Other utensils should include a can opener, bottle opener, and a cork screw (you never know!). Use your multi-tool pliers to handle hot pots and pans which don't have handles.

I take a small backpacking grill (seen in the picture above) in case I want to make popcorn over the campfire. That little grill came in handy once when our only propane tank failed due to a clogged hose. One trick to keep your pots and pans from blackening over a campfire is to lightly coat the outside with soap. The soot and ash will wash off easily.

Coolers

This is one of my favorite topics because the difference between a cheap vs. quality cooler and good cooler usage habits can make the difference as to whether you will be able to enjoy foods that must otherwise stay refrigerated. The more expensive coolers will have fully insulated sides, an insulated bottom, and an insulated lid which seals well. Bigger is not necessarily better.

Bigger just means you'll have to feed it more ice, and of course bigger takes up more space. I like the 40 to 50 quart size. I can carry several of them, and on longer trips use one just for ice so anything requiring refrigeration will last an extra day or two.

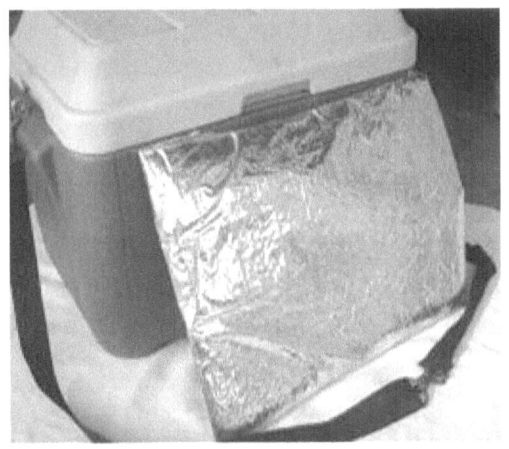

A couple of tips for coolers; many coolers lids' are not insulated. I bought a couple of cans of compressed insulating material, drilled a ¼ inch hole at either end of the underside of the lid, and filled the lid with the insulation. I also filled the cup holders too. Next, I bought some insulating pads for air conditioners, cut to the size of the cooler. I cut up one of those Mylar "Space Blankets" and made a sleeve in which to insert the insulating pad. Placing the insulation pad on the top of the cooler full of ice and provisions will help make the ice last longer.

As the ice melts, and the contents of the cooler settle, the insulating pad will settle as well. The ice is cooling only the part of the cooler containing provisions, not all the empty space at the top.

If you are camping in warmer climate, I suggest setting coolers in the shade. Place each cooler on a couple of strips of wood (or whatever is convenient) to keep them off the hot ground.

Tip: If the lid on your cooler doesn't close all the way, seal it using insulation strips. Use the type where one side peels off exposing an adhesive. The strips will last longer if you apply them underneath the lid.

If you have the option, replenish your coolers with ice instead of leaving half-ice and half-water. And if possible, use block ice instead of, or in addition to, ice cubes because block ice lasts longer and is usually cheaper. I use an old hatchet to split block ice into a few smaller pieces for distributing into each of the coolers.

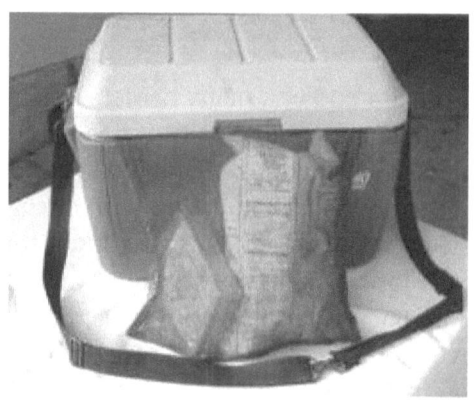

As far as I know, there are no laws against making modifications to your equipment. One of the things I got tired of was hauling a "day cooler" down to the water from my campsite. Not only are they not large enough for all of the drinks and snacks for the day, they are typically not efficient and waste ice. Shown above is a forty quart cooler in which I drilled a hole in either side, secured a couple of eye bolts, and attached a strap I had saved from some previous equipment failure.

I can sling this over my shoulder which allows me to carry my inner tube and umbrella down to the shore all in one trip. By the way, save stuff bags, straps, and other accessories from all discarded equipment that may be of use later. I once repaired one of my tents by replacing a zipper which had snapped. A few minutes of repair work saved me 100 bucks on a new tent.

Tip: Attach a netted carrying bag like the type used for carrying sports equipment to the side of your cooler. It's a handy way to pack your sun screen, camera, and your favorite snacks that don't have to be refrigerated.

The cooler pictured above is used primarily for day trips to the beach or to bring lunch to work. Note the cover is basically a sheet of thick plastic with no insulation, very inefficient, and wastes ice. The cooler body swivels underneath the handle and is secured only by a plastic spring-loaded button. The first and last time I used this type of cooler the button wore out. Being spring loaded the button and spring shot out like a cannon ball never to be seen again. The body of the cooler swung open, and my lunch ended up all over the driveway.

Dry Ice

Dry ice, which is frozen carbon dioxide, has a freezing point of about 100 degrees below zero. Dry ice does not melt to liquid water like regular ice. Dry ice sublimates, or evaporates as a gas. I have found the biggest advantage for using dry ice is to preserve regular ice for a couple more days before having to replenish my supply. The downside is you will burn your hands handling dry ice unless you use gloves. Keep all dry ice away from the little campers. You must also be careful not to keep anything containing dry ice in an enclosed area (like your vehicle). Remember, dry ice evaporates as carbon dioxide which displaces oxygen in an enclosed area. Breathing excessive amounts of carbon dioxide will result in oxygen deprivation causing potential serious health risks.

I've bought dry ice for as little as $1.00 per pound. Dry ice is more expensive than regular ice, but depending on what the nearest store to your campsite charges for ice, how much gas are you going to use to get to the store, and how much time you spend away from your camping trip might justify the extra initial expense. Dry ice is often packaged in blocks about a third the size of a regular block if ice. Wrapping dry ice in newspaper allows for excellent insulation, and you don't want dry ice to come in direct contact with other packages, food, water, or regular ice. If you intend to keep food items frozen, or for preserving regular ice as I described above, place the dry ice on top of the coolers' contents.

The key to using dry ice is cold air sinks to the bottom of the cooler. If you just want to keep items like beverages cool, then place the dry ice on the bottom of the cooler followed by a layer of regular ice. Another precaution is not to let dry ice come into direct contact with the cooler itself.

Dry ice is so cold it will cause the plastic inside your cooler to crack. Cut up a Styrofoam cooler and place the pieces in between the bottom and sides of the cooler and the dry ice. And, leaving a canned beverage directly on dry ice is like leaving it in the freezer at home, it's going to expand and burst!

You made have heard a few other tales of woe about the use of dry ice. I'm guessing one of them has to do with a "funny" taste in any food stored along with dry ice, and another describes cooler lids launching off into deep space. While I have never had any funny tasting food as a result of using dry ice, I do take the extra precaution of leaving the drain plug open and the latches unsecured on any cooler containing dry ice. This allows the carbon dioxide gas as a result of the dry ice evaporating to escape preventing the lid from popping open. This is especially true for me since I've modified my coolers with extra insulation and weather stripping around the edge of the lids to ensure a tighter seal.

Note: If you need to break the dry ice block, use the hammer end your hatchet and tap a tent stake (number two nail which I describe later). A hatchet with a hammer end saves having to pack a regular hammer.

Based on my experience, ten pounds of dry ice in a decent fifty quart cooler will keep about six blocks of regular ice frozen for about three days assuming daytime high temperatures of as much as 105 degrees. And there is still enough ice after five days to maintain a small cooler. These results also assume you have taken advantage of the tips about managing coolers and ice as described earlier.

Tip: By the way, try to limit the how often coolers are opened. Each time the lid is open, you allow hot air from the outside to replace the cool air from inside causing the ice to melt quicker.

Comparison

On another trip in early September in the Southern Sierra Nevada Mountains, typically one of the hottest times of the year, I packed my coolers exactly as I did when I used dry ice. Except this time I did not use dry ice. The purpose was to compare how well dry ice works in general. However, that year was an unexpected exception. Daytime temperatures averaged only about 85 degrees throughout the week, nighttime temperatures dropped as low as 54 degrees making average temperatures for an entire 24 hour day about 70 degrees. The much cooler temperatures are a big boost for keeping perishable items from spoiling on a longer trip not to mention not having to replenish your ice as often.

By comparison, on the final full day of our July trip using dry ice, we actually had a few fist-sized pieces of ice, still useful, which amazingly made it through the entire week. On the September trip, we had only remnants of ice after the third day. Since our September trip was noticeably cooler than the July trip, and the fact the ice lasted only a few days rather than the entire week, proves dry ice to be an excellent method of preserving regular ice for as much as three or four extra days.

A couple more notes about using dry ice. If you use dry ice to freeze food such as steaks, hot dogs, or cold cuts, you'll need to allow additional time for thawing. Remember, dry ice freezes at almost 100 degrees below zero so foods will "super cool" as well. You will likely notice the dry ice evaporating within a day or two after initially packing your cooler. That's okay because what's really happened is that the regular ice has super-cooled which is what allows it to last longer.

Games

Bocce Ball, Badminton, Volley Ball, and Horseshoes are great for the kids after a day's hike. I also take a couple of board games, dominos, and a deck of playing cards just in case the weather keeps us under the shade or in the tent for awhile. I always take a Frisbee and a couple of kites, too.

Lanterns

I have used a lantern perhaps once in the past twenty years or so, but I do pack one just in case. The last time I used one was only because we didn't get back to camp until after dark, and the lantern made it easier to fix dinner.

I like the Coleman dual mantle propane lantern shown below. The top section conveniently screws directly to the propane bottle which also serves as part of the lantern assembly. The bottom of the propane bottle is seated in a plastic base. I always carry several extra mantles.

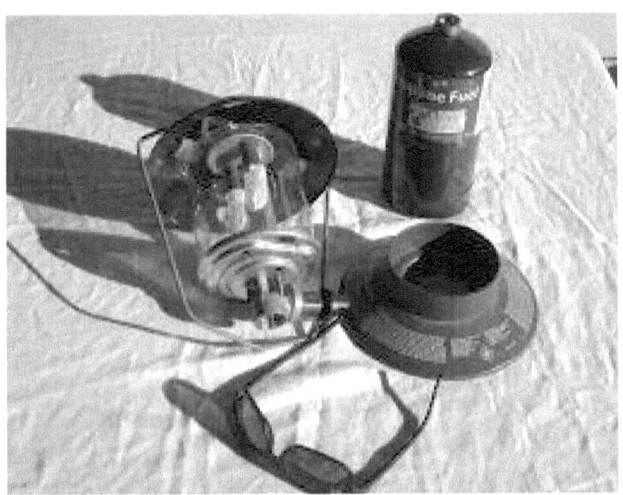

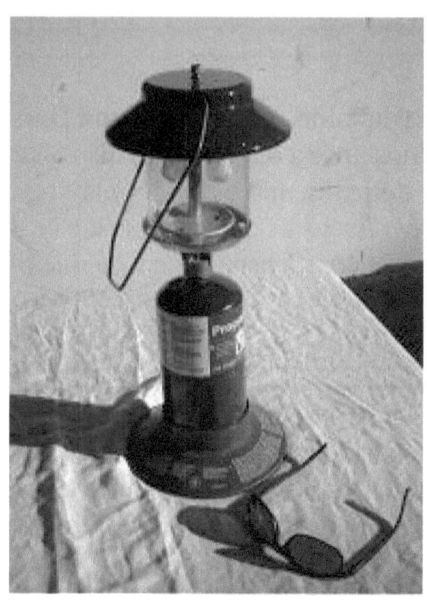

I also carry an extra globe, just in case. I like this particular model because it uses 16.4 ounce propane bottles, and they are easy pack and store. One bottle averages eight to ten hours of lighting time depending on how high you set the flame. The same type of propane bottle may used with the stove as well.

Replacing the mantle is easy. The mantle is a small sock made of a cloth-like material. It has a draw string at one end. Simply tighten the draw string around the grooved end of the tube carrying the propane from the bottle into the mantle and tie it off. Unfortunately, there's not a lot of room to work with, so I get one of my campers with smaller hands to do this for me rather than risk damaging a mantle.

Shade, Canopies, Umbrellas

Beach umbrellas are just that, for the beach. They are difficult to anchor, and in a primitive camping environment where wind gusts can easily reach 30 or 40 mph, they can take off like a rocket. I've come close to getting impaled by beach umbrellas more than once.

I do however, like the umbrella concept. But the type of umbrella I use is the same type you find around the association pool. These are built to withstand the elements, as they obviously are outside most of the time. They are typically anchored in a cast iron or concrete base. I have this type of umbrella and base (shown below) and I use it for minimal shade requirements such as down by the lake or river. Note the small section of steel tubing welded to a C-clamp along with a couple of eye bolts which screw into threaded nuts on the side. When attached to a picnic bench, for example, you shouldn't have to secure the umbrella base with additional weight.

Use sun screen even if you plan to stay under your collapsible shade or umbrella. If it is overcast, ultraviolet light (UV) not only penetrates cloud cover, but can also penetrate most shade material. Use sun screen around water to prevent sun burn from the reflected sun light.

I also recommend equipping each camper with their own personal umbrella with a clamp (shown below attached to the camp chair) for protection from both rain and sun. Before purchasing personal umbrellas, check for any UV or wind gust ratings which may help you decide which type to buy.

By far, the worst types of alternatives for shade are the $29.00 canopies sold in discount stores requiring you to stake down a couple of guy lines per leg. These are flimsy, and are of no practical use for camping. I couldn't convince a friend of mine though.

I watched for a couple of hours as he struggled with setting up his bargain canopy. I can't remember laughing harder when almost as soon as he was done setting this thing up, a sudden gust of wind instantly turned his canopy into a kite. All said and done, he laughed too!

The best shade options are the collapsible canopies which fit into roughly a 1 foot by 1 foot by 5 foot carrying case. (By the way, this is one piece of equipment where the carrying case is actually useable beyond just the first time). They are easy to setup and take down, even by only one person. The height is adjustable in 3 or 4 increments of perhaps a foot or so.

Collapsible canopies are usually advertised in sizes based on the number of square feet of coverage, and understanding the actual amount of shade provided can be deceiving. A canopy advertised as 10 feet by 10 feet may actually be the dimensions between the bottoms of each leg. The actual amount of shade depends on the size of the tarp that secures to the top of the frame which may be 8 feet by 8 feet, the size I prefer. Larger canopies are not any more rugged, yet they require more anchoring, thus are more at risk of being damaged if the wind decides to get busy.

To set up the canopy, gently shake and pull the leg at each corner apart a little at a time taking care none of the linkage of the canopy frame gets tangled during this process.

After you have expanded the linkage all the way, secure the corner at the top of each leg by seating the spring-loaded retaining pin into the hole (shown above). You can see each spring loaded pin has a ring to allow you to pull the pin when you are ready to collapse the canopy.

The picture above shows how the retaining pin secures from inside the canopy. After the corners of the canopy cover are secured by Velcro at the top of the legs, expand the legs to the desired length. The legs "telescope" whereby the bottom half of the leg slides out from inside the top half, and is secured by a spring loaded retaining pin.

There are three or four holes about a foot apart along each leg allowing you to choose the height at which you would like to set your canopy.

Located under the canopy in the middle of each corner will be a Velcro fastener. Secure the fastener to the canopy frame. This insures the canopy will not blow off the frame.

So, what's the first thing you do when you bring your new canopy home? (Hint: same as your new tent, discussed later). Toss the stakes that came with it. In fact, don't even use stakes to anchor your canopy. Instead, buy some heavy gauge sheet metal and cut four 1 foot by 1 foot plates (one for each leg), and drill a 3/8 inch hole in a corner of each plate. Buy four sets of nuts, bolts, and washers. Secure the bottom of each leg of the canopy to a plate using a nut, bolt, and washers. Stack rocks on each of the plates. You'll get what I mean when you see all of the campground dumpsters full of canopy skeletons because they weren't sufficiently anchored.

If you're going to the beach, where there likely are no large rocks, substitute the plates with plastic buckets. After fastening each leg to a hole drilled in the bottom center of a bucket, simply fill with sand. I wouldn't take a chance on using tent stakes (described later in this guide); tent stakes are intended for soft ground, not beach sand. As shown in the picture above, I have filled a bucket with several smaller rocks and placed the bucket on the plate. You can also see where the bottom of one of the legs of the canopy is secured to the plate with a nut and bolt, and a couple of washers. I recall on this particular trip I clocked wind gusts just over forty miles an hour, and had no problems with the canopy.

Tip: Create larger shade areas by overlapping a couple of canopies together where the legs cross about mid way. Wire ties work great for lashing together canopy legs.

Canopies are available with many accessories. Shown below is a 10 x 10 collapsible canopy including four walls made of mosquito netting and two solid nylon walls to act as a windbreak. This particular model also came with guy lines for securing the top of each leg to a stake in the ground for added strength.

In addition to protection from sun and rain, bringing your own shade often gives you more choices for a great camp spot. Most people will opt for the campsites with the most shade trees which may not actually be the nicest spot in the campground. I like, for example, campsites that have easier access to the river or lake. And while they may not have a lot of trees for shade, I'm also avoiding the natural consequences of birds, tree sap, and falling tree branches.

Shower, Outdoor

Basically, the outdoor shower is a tent about 5 feet by 5 feet, and about 7 feet high with no floor. Use the same staking method described for tents (a little later) for both the shower and shower's guy lines. The low spot, or basin, in your campsite is an ideal place to setup your outdoor shower. As I discuss a little later, the low spot is not where you want to setup your tent anyway.

There is a "shelf" that is actually a net secured inside the shower over your head. This is where you place the shower bladder. The bladder is a flexible plastic or rubber container, similar to a hot water bottle, and is filled with a couple of gallons of water. There is a hose with a shower head which is easily opened and closed when taking your shower.

Place the bladder in the net overhead with the shower head accessible. Depending on the season, you may want to lay the bladders (I suggest having more than one) in direct sunlight to warm the water. Be careful though, this can work too good as the water can heat to scalding hot.

Tip: you can buy incandescent (glow in the dark) clips which attach to guy lines if you're prone like me for not watching where you're going…

Sleeping Bags

If you plan to camp in conditions outside of the minimum temperature range which I established at the beginning of this guide, then my recommendations on sleeping bags do not apply. For conditions above the minimum temperature, I recommend sleeping bags rated for at least 40 degrees Fahrenheit. These don't have to be expensive, perhaps $20 to $30. I recommend purchasing pairs of sleeping bags that are exactly the same. In colder weather identical sleeping bags can be zipped together allowing several of the little campers to share a bag so they will stay warmer. I also highly recommend bringing a couple of extra bags in case you have to double bag (placing one sleeping bag inside another) if it gets too cold.

I only bring blankets on summer trips when I know it's likely to remain warm throughout the night, and when a sleeping bag would be too hot. If you have purchased the appropriate bags for colder weather camping, blankets should not be necessary, and they are bulky and difficult to pack.

Tip: rather than bringing pillows, pack unused clothing and coats into the sleeping bag stuff bags for use as pillows.

There are perhaps as many different types of sleeping bags as tents, and purchasing the right sleeping bag can be a challenge. The type I recommended above typically weighs about four pounds and is approximately 3 feet wide by about 6 1/2 feet long. The filling and lining is usually made of 100% Polyester.

Sleeping bags rated for below freezing conditions are going to be considerably more expensive. These bags are generally filled using duck or goose down (feathers), the zippers are insulated and do not zip the entire length of the bag (which helps retain heat), and are sewn together using a "box" type construction. Box construction means there are no seams completely sewn through both the inner and outer lining, again to preserve body heat. These types of sleeping bags are often referred to as "mummy" bags because they are not rectangular in shape but are tapered towards the bottom to save weight and improve performance. I have several mummy bags, and although they do their job extremely well, they are confining. And unless it's cold out, they're just too uncomfortably warm.

Sleeping Pads

I've tried most every type of sleeping pad, and all have advantages and disadvantages. Air mattresses can be comfortable, but there is a lot of movement every time the camper you're sharing a mattress with changes position. Sleeping on an air mattress is much like sleeping on a water bed. Air mattresses often leak and become nothing more than a thick ground cloth by morning. They require the use of a pump, which of course means you need batteries. This presents a situation that if any of the components fail, and you have no backup plan, you are not going to achieve one of the themes of this guide – comfort. If you or your camping companions are not comfortable, you're less likely to have an enjoyable trip.

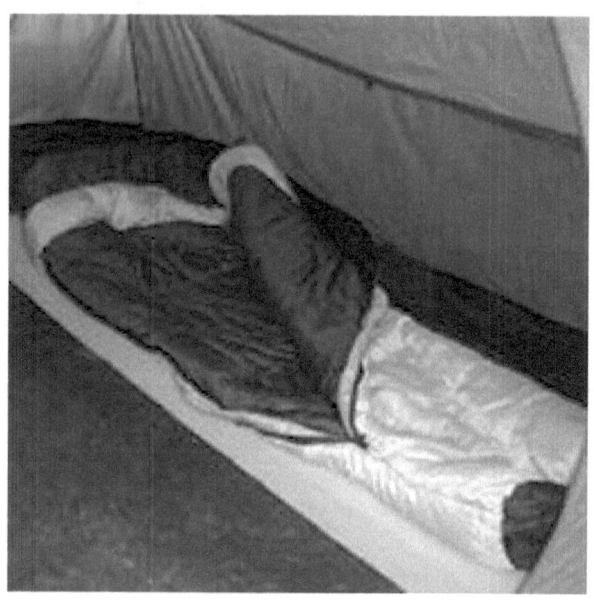

Compressed foam pads offer some thermal protection and they are better than nothing. Keep in mind sleeping pads double duty as insulation from the ground as well as to provide comfort. I save the compressed foam pads for use when backpacking.

You can purchase "self-inflating" sleeping pads. Actually, they are made with standard foam and sealed in a durable nylon sleeve. When you unroll it and open the valve, the foam expands to about an inch thick. These pads are far better, but they are expensive.

What do I use? Nothing more than foam padding scavenged from an old couch or foam mattress (shown above). I prefer a pad about six feet by 3 feet by at least 2 inches. They're a pain to roll up and strap, but the extra work is worth it to me. I have a couple of larger duffle bags which I use to pack all of the foam sleeping pads.

Cots

One alternative to sleeping pads and air mattresses is a cot. And, I'm not talking about the old canvas and wood Army cots which weighed a ton and took a day to set up. Modern cots made of nylon and aluminum frame are light and easy to assemble.

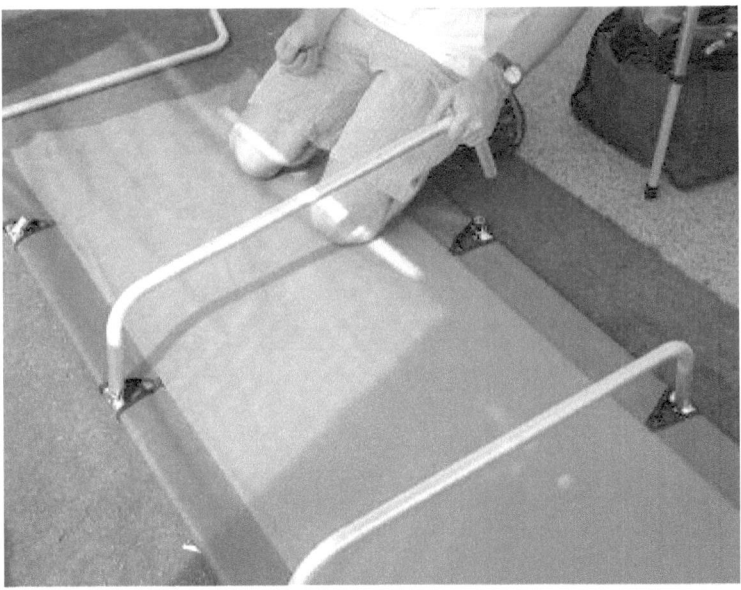

I think the greatest advantage to using a cot over pads and mattresses is you are completely off the ground by several inches thus avoiding sleeping on uneven ground and protruding rocks. And if you do unknowingly setup your tent in catch basin during a few showers, you're more likely stay dry.

If you go with the cot configuration, be sure to acquire only the type with "U" shaped legs which distributes the weight such that your tent floor will not get punctured. I also recommend using a sleeping pad on top of the cot because you will still need insulation and some padding to be comfortable.

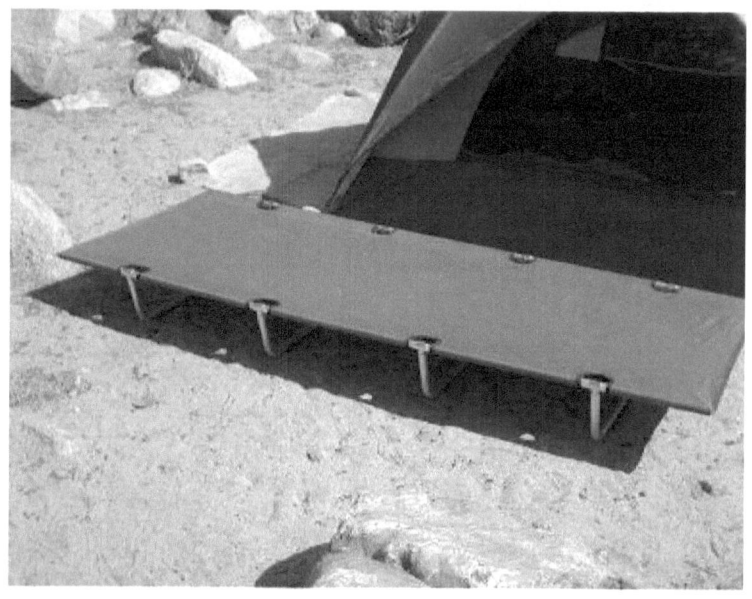

Stove

Simple is best. I like the two-burner propane model made by Coleman. It's lightweight, easy to setup, has a convenient handle, and folds into the size of a briefcase for easy packing and storage.

I can take or leave any make or model stove with piezo ignition (also commonly referred to as "matchless" ignition). The concept is great, and when it works it's wonderful. But I have found piezo ignition to be somewhat temperamental. It's not 100% reliable and I'm not sure if it's because of ambient temperature, humidity, altitude, or some combination thereof. Anyway, a butane barbeque lighter works just fine. I like using the 16.4 ounce propane bottles as they are easy pack and store.

One bottle averages about an hour of cooking time with both burners set on high.

Keep in mind a quart of water boils in about 4 to 5 minutes (depending on altitude). I recommend packing at least one 16.4 ounce propane bottle per day per 4 campers, and take a couple extra if you're going for a week or more.

If you have room to spare, rigging a 2½ or five gallon propane tank will take all the guess work out of whether you'll have enough fuel. Regardless of how you configure your propane stove, always test it before your trip. Propane lines can deteriorate, clog, and fail, and the larger bottles provide a false sense of security. In other words, it's easier to run out of gas using a five gallon bottle than packing several new small bottles. Note the "T" adapter on the five gallon bottle pictured above which allows fueling more than one appliance at a time.

Tables

If you are going to a developed campground, it's likely you'll have the standard picnic table available for use. I usually set my shade up over the picnic table, and it becomes the center of most activity. When primitive camping (for me that means going miles off road and finding a spot with nothing more than a view and some flat ground to set up a tent), I carry a small collapsible table for placement in between camp chairs, a larger collapsible table suitable for the stove and cooking equipment, and a fold-up card table which serves as the classic picnic table.

Tents

Back in the days when I did a lot of cross country backpacking using topographic maps and a compass, I packed something called a Tube Tent. It was nothing more than a cylinder, or tube of heavy plastic, cost only a couple of bucks, and weighed under two pounds. I used it primarily as a ground cloth, but in bad weather I could string cord through it, set rocks in the inside corners, and tie off each end of the cord to a couple of trees. When above the tree line, I simply used a fishing pole on one end secured by a couple of guy lines (cordage anchored using stakes). I folded the other end and secured with rocks

Tents which can be purchased today, even the cheapest that are nothing more than nylon with a couple of fiber glass poles, were not generally available back then. And, if you could find them, they cost well into the hundreds, even thousands of dollars. I am going into some detail here because your tent is one of your most important pieces of equipment.

I prefer the simple dome tent, perhaps the most common. Two fiber glass poles for the tent itself (the kind with the elastic in the middle of the pole holding each section for easy setup and breakdown), with a third pole for the rain fly. The larger the diameter of the poles, the sturdier the tent will be. While I've been in wind conditions with gusts up to 50 mph, the tent type I am describing is good for perhaps 20 to 25 mph, comfortably that is. Worst case scenario is to tie off where the poles intersect at the top of the tent into the wind to a tree, rock, or your vehicle. I find this a particularly good idea when camping on the beach. You could also place other camping equipment on each of the inside corners of the tent for additional anchoring.

Note: The rain fly also helps insulate the tent for warmth in addition to protection from rain.

Important tip: Tent size is obviously important and depends on who, and how many, are going to use a given tent. When a tent says it will accommodate "X" number of persons, always subtract at least one to get a more realistic number. Subtract one more if you plan to store equipment in the tent. I prefer a size I can stand in almost all the way up allowing me to change clothes with relative privacy and without having to bend over. By default, this usually means the tent will comfortably sleep 3 adults, depending on how much equipment is stored in the tent.

I prefer to pack several of these sized tents, one for my wife and myself, one for the tweens, and one for my teenage niece. This might seem a little bit obsessive-compulsive, but the real reason is I like to have an extra tent for emergencies, plus everyone has to set their own tent up and break it down without my help anyway, except for my role as supervisor of course! Seriously, teaching the kids to perform camping duties on their own is a valuable learning experience. Obviously, you're not going to allow a four year old to handle a hatchet or a knife, but assign tasks based on age and skill level.

The second thing you do when purchasing a new tent (I'll tell you the first thing in a bit) is to purchase a stuff bag or equipment bag at least 30% larger than that of the bag which came with the new tent. I guarantee you will never get the new tent back into the stuff bag it came with. But save the bag in case you need it for a smaller tent. I recommend storing the "stakes" in a tool box, or someplace where they will not come into contact with the tents.

New tents should be set up at home prior to use in the field to make sure there are no tears in the material and that it came with all the poles and the rain fly. Not to mention so you'll have some idea of how to set it up when you get to your campsite.

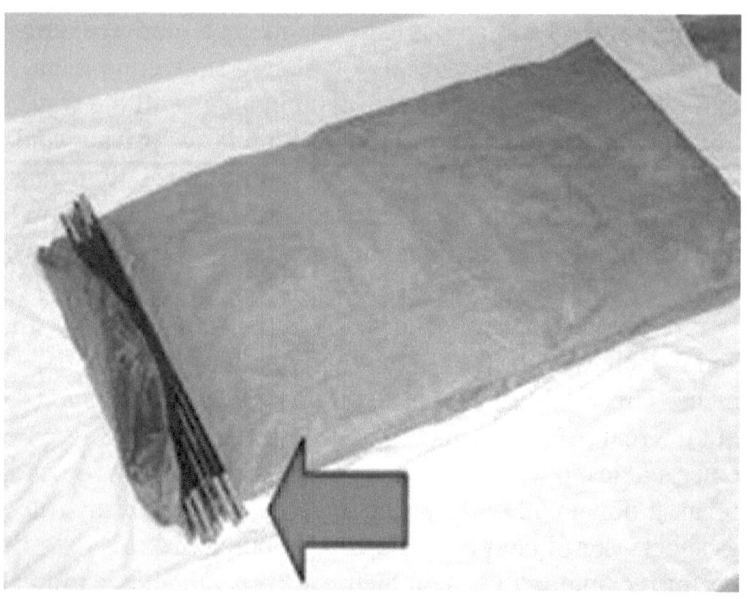

Here's an excellent tip on packing your tent: fold the tent, including the rain fly, into quarters or thirds (whatever is convenient to fit the equipment bag you bought for it), and use the poles to roll the tent around. Rolling the tent around the poles provides extra rigidity making the tent easier to stuff in the equipment bag, and you're less likely to lose the poles or mix the poles up with other tents.

Shown above is my smaller "backup" tent folded into quarters by width, and folded in half by length with the rain fly included. I've placed the two tent poles and the rain fly pole at the loose end.

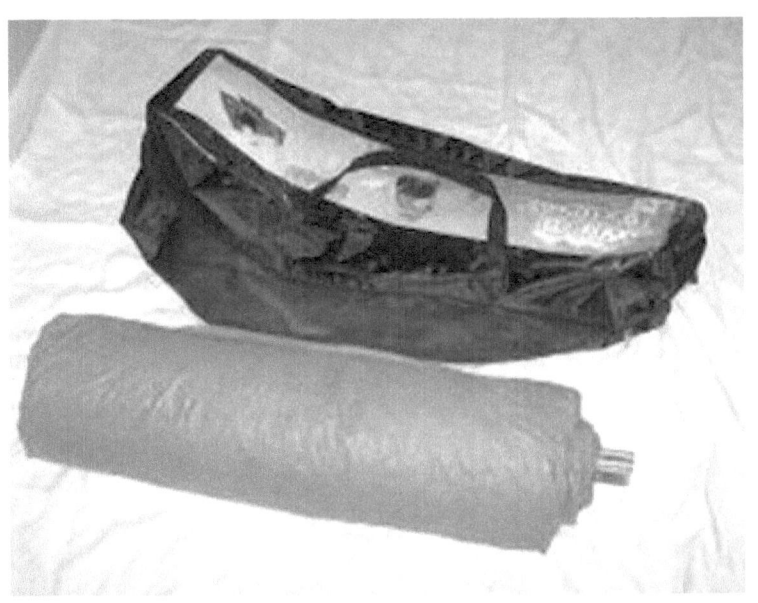

While rolling up the tent dust off excess soil and let all air out. The end result will easily fit in the bag. I suggest keeping the picture that came with the tent attached to the stuff bag (as seen here) so the kids have something to reference while they are setting it up.

Other Tent Types

There are many tent styles to choose from. This one pictured above is part tent, part cot. One of the advantages to this configuration is you're up off the ground which solves the problem of ending up sleeping in a catch basin if it rains. Another big advantage is "ease of use". This tent unfolds like a table and sets up in just a few minutes. This tent type provides excellent insulation, and in fact the United States military used this particular model for our armed forces in Iraq and Afghanistan. The only drawbacks are cost (a bit out of my budget), and it's a little awkward to transport.

The type of tent pictured here is often referred to as a "swag" tent. The swag tent originated in Australia and New Zealand and is still among the most preferred tent types for use in the Australian Outback. Swag tents typically include a sewn in sleeping pad, are made of water proof canvas, and are easy to setup and take down. I especially like the low profile design which adds much greater shelter from high winds. Note in this picture a lean-to made of lightweight nylon has been added just to allow the swag tent to thoroughly dry quicker in the event of rain.

Tent Repair

You may have noticed a little emergency field repair applied to the dome tent in the picture a couple of pages ago. On one trip, we encountered unusually heavy wind gusts during the previous night which tore the tie-down (metal ring) from one corner of the tent. Fortunately, the rain fly was secured enough to prevent further damage to the tent. As a temporary fix, I placed a golf ball size rock all the way into the inside corner of the tent (the red arrow to right). I looped a length of cordage around the "neck" created by the rock inside the tent corner. This is a technique known as "button-holing". I secured the other end of the cordage through a loop tied around the double stakes (arrow at left). This is also an excellent opportunity for you to see the taunt line knot (arrow at center, see also Appendix D) and the method for double staking.

You can see here I drove the stakes through the tie-down in opposite directions, in an "X" shape. An equipment failure is going to occur at the weakest link in the chain, in this case it was the stitching of the tie down to the tent which was easy to fix once back at home.

Button-holing can be used in a variety of situations. I mentioned earlier about using plastic tube tents many years ago when backpacking. Tying off a small stone on the top of each end of the tube tent allowed me to secure the tube tent to fishing poles in place of tent poles when I was above the tree line. The same technique works well for securing tarps and space blankets when using as part of an emergency shelter.

Field Test: Three Season Tent

On one particular outing to the infamous Mojave Desert in Southern California, I learned more about having the right equipment for appropriate conditions. Although it was late fall, the desert is still a fascinating environment. I enjoy spending hours just gazing at the colors of the surrounding mountains and the desert floor as day turns to evening. Even though the desert is peaceful most of the time, weather can turn on a dime. The infamous Santa Ana winds can pack punches well beyond category 1 hurricane force winds, though usually gusts of forty to fifty miles an hour are more common. On this trip I field tested a "three season" family size tent with the floor measuring 13 by 9 feet and a height of about 6 ½ feet.

Note: The term "three season" is a rating of sorts meaning the equipment is designed for the spring, summer, and fall seasons. Notice winter is not included.

The tent I tested is luxurious by my standards, and it can be configured for two rooms, each having its own entrance. There is easily enough space in each room for three adults, a small table, and even a couple of chairs. The tent is easy to set up and take down with two people, but it does weigh a hefty 50 pounds or so. There are only four poles easily assembled because of the elastic cord connecting each section of each pole. The poles themselves are made of ¾ inch aluminum and should be able to withstand the specifications for which it was designed.

Ironically, I end up learning something every time I go camping. And, not necessarily the good stuff. This time I learned it's not a good idea to use a high profile tent in gale force winds. This is one of the peak times of the year for the Santa Ana winds in this part of the state, and I managed to plan this outing right at the onset. Santa Ana winds are caused by a massive high pressure system which envelops much of Utah and Nevada pushing hot air through Southern California. In addition to the high winds and warmer temperatures, humidity can drop below double digits. Santa Ana conditions are largely responsible for the propagation of wild fires.

My first mistake was not anchoring the tent properly. As I discuss later in this guide, there are many types of stakes which can be used depending on the circumstances. High desert camping is similar to camping on the beach, except the ground is not quite as soft. Even so, I didn't properly stake this tent for these conditions. The end result was I had to physically hold the tent by one of the poles while my wife, daughter, nieces, and nephew re-staked the tent and anchored it from the inside. Unfortunately that effort was too little, too late.

A sudden strong gust pulled the tent away from me so hard that the tent pole snapped in my hand. I did manage to salvage the situation by applying some simple field repairs, namely a splint using spare fiberglass tent poles and duct tape. Next time, I will hold the tent by the corner seam.

Replacement Parts

The next important lesson I learned was making sure replacement parts are available for all my camping and emergency preparedness equipment. Yet another unfortunate part of this story – the tent manufacturer does not provide replacement poles for models using aluminum poles. Nor have I been able to find replacement poles anywhere else. This surprised even me as the tent manufacturer is a well known brand. The tent retails for about $600.00.

Ultimately, I resolved the problem by going to the hardware store and buying a section of 5/8 inch steel conduit to slide inside the section of broken tent pole. The repair, although a bit inconvenient, is a viable long term solution. And, I now bring a spare section of conduit just in case.

The moral to this story is: don't use equipment rated for three seasons in four season conditions, and make sure the manufacturer of any equipment you make a significant investment in provides replacement parts.

Tent Stakes

The very first thing you do with a new tent is throw away
the cheap plastic or wire tent stakes that came with it:

Then go to the hardware store and buy a dozen 3/8 inch by 12 inch nails like these shown here:

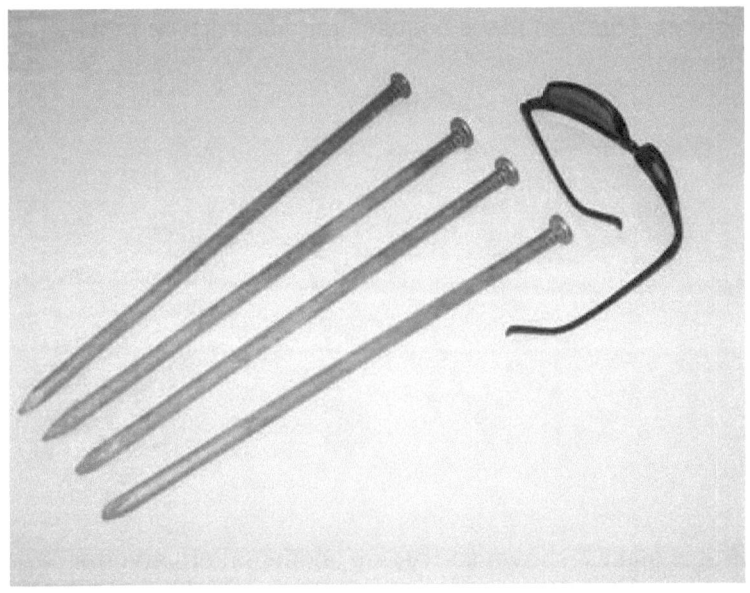

Watching newbie's "tent chasing" races is absolutely delightful, it's just I'd rather be a spectator and not a participant. In addition to staking your tent down with my recommended replacement stakes, I also suggest propping a large rock on top of each stake. If you're expecting any wind, double stake each corner of the tent by driving each pair in an "X" pattern.

For soft sand areas, such as the desert, I recommend the same size stakes, but with a triangular piece of heavy gauge sheet metal welded towards the top of the stake (shown above). This acts like a boat anchor when driven into soft ground.

Auger stakes (shown above) are another alternative for staking down in soft ground, but they are a bit more work.

Staking a tent at the beach is usually much more challenging. I drive two foot lengths of conduit into the sand to secure each corner of the tent.

Tools

While I always carry a set of tools which allow me to
perform many basic emergency vehicle repairs, the
minimum for comfortable camping should include the
following:

Cutting axe
Hatchet
Knife
Multi-tool
Rake
Shovel
Wisk broom

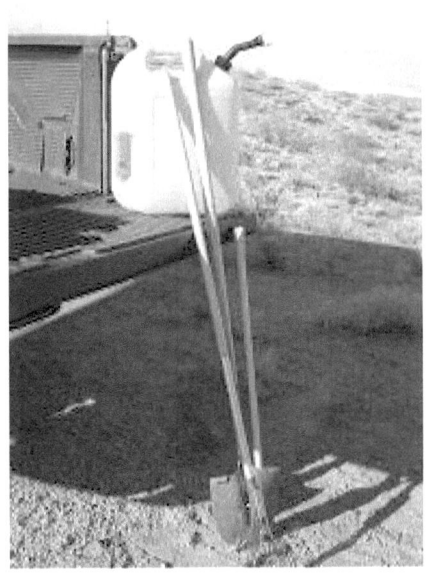

I consider the ax, hatchet, and shovel mandatory. The broom and rake is self explanatory, though worth mentioning just in case. The ax is obviously used for splitting firewood. The hatchet can be used for both splitting firewood and as a hammer to drive tent stakes.

I always bring my own firewood (purchased locally and indigenous to the area I am visiting so as not to transport hitchhiking insects). And, buying firewood discourages irresponsible campers from picking the forests clean of dead wood, live tree branches, and other plants. However, I once got stuck in my four-wheel drive vehicle such that the very center point of the skid plate was all that was in contact with a rather large boulder. Needless to say, the ax came in very handy for cutting lengths of branches for forcing traction since none of the four wheels were in contact with the ground.

On another occasion, we arrived at our camping spot just before sunup. I parked my four wheel drive vehicle on the snow which was, of course, frozen. I learned the hard way snow does melt, which left us stuck. Although we planned to camp for several days and would not need the vehicle during that time, we worked throughout the day to dig a path and line with branches for additional traction when the snow was again frozen the following morning. I was able to get the vehicle out of the snow and back onto hard ground.

Shown above is a 6 gallon water jug, the type I recommend for any trip. In fact I have a half-dozen of these I store at home in the event of an emergency. I usually take one jug on camping trips lasting 2 or 3 nights, two jugs if the trip is longer. Note the convenient spout which collapses into the jug itself when not in use preventing damage.

The blue color of the jug is intentional indicating the jug is for water only. Never use a blue jug for gasoline or anything else but water. Never use any jug for any content other than what it is rated for.

Duct Tape

Duct tape deserves its' own section for discussion. Duct tape can mean the difference between success and failure of an entire trip. Duct tape has an infinite number of uses, for example, I've used duct tape as a temporary repair on tent poles which had snapped. I used duct tape to effect temporary repair of my favorite pair of river sandals (the sole had split), and they lasted the rest of the trip. Tearing in the floor or walls of your tent can easily be temporarily repaired by applying a length of duct tape on both sides allowing the adhesive sides of the tape to adhere. In the picture below I show one way of temporarily repairing a snapped tent pole. Place two lengths of a broom stick, or spare tent pole, alongside the part of the pole which snapped, and apply the tape. This is called a splint, and should last the rest of the trip.

Tip: I recommend folding over the end of the tape on the roll about a quarter inch making it much easier to find and pull the end of the tape the next time you need to use it.

Fire Extinguisher

This is an optional piece of equipment, but I highly recommend purchasing a 10lb ABC unit. The ABC designation means the fire extinguisher is effective for electrical, grease, flammable liquids, and paper and wood fueled fire. Don't waste your money on the cheap plastic kitchen models and prepare for a price tag of around $100.00. Remember, this piece of equipment can be a life saver on your camping trips, but it can do double duty in the event of a kitchen fire at home.

Follow the instructions printed on the outside of the fire extinguisher. The extinguisher contains a dry chemical combined with a compressed propellant. I have (fortunately) only had to use mine a couple times. One time worth noting was when I happened upon a driver who had crashed head on into a large tree. I checked on the driver and thankfully, it was a low speed impact and he was okay. Meanwhile the engine compartment had caught fire and was beginning to spread to a large pine tree.

This was in a dangerous location, in dry forested area, relatively well populated. I decided not to attempt to put the fire out, but instead I hit the spots on the tree at the base of the flame which were igniting with short bursts of the dry chemical. I was able to keep the fire contained to the car for about 10 minutes. And that was perfect timing as the fire department arrived just as I had emptied my extinguisher. Smaller extinguishers, such as this 10 pound model, come equipped with mounting hardware. If you can't use the mounting hardware for you vehicle, make sure you store it so the pressure gauge cannot be sheared off. And, of course, you don't want the handle mechanism to accidentally deploy.

Flashlight

Another important investment is your flashlight. Odds are you won't need it much if you can accustom yourself to seeing by starlight (or moonlight). I use a technique called averted vision which allows you to see using peripheral vision rather than focusing on an object directly with the eye. I'll let you research averted vision on your own. It takes a bit of practice but comes in real handy. (Hint: if you can count the number of stars in the Pleiades constellation without the help of binoculars or a telescope, you have learned to use averted vision).This is also one of the reasons I don't generally use a lantern. If you have ever watched amateur astronomers in the field, you've probably wondered why they use only light with red filters. This helps their eyes adjust enabling viewing of the night sky through telescopes while intermittently referring to star charts, computer screens, and the like.

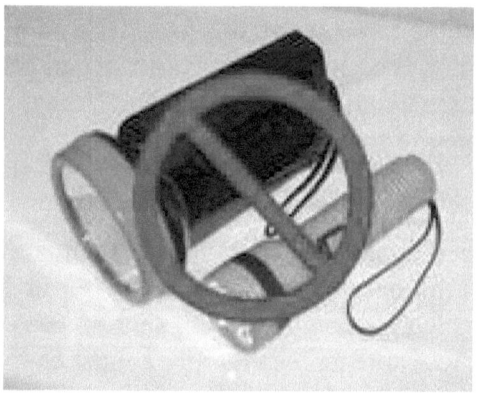

I've tried many different types of flashlights and prefer the models shown below made by MagLite. They are made of aluminum, are extremely durable, and generate more than adequate lighting. Don't bother with cheap plastic flashlights, like the kind sold as a promotion along with batteries. They won't last one outing.

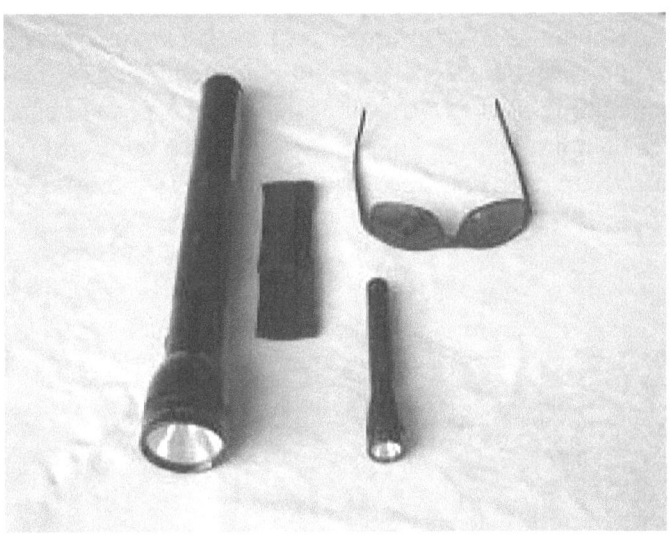

The sunglasses have been placed next to the flashlights to give you some perspective as to size. The larger flashlight is a four cell "D" size, while the smaller is a two cell "AA" size. Both are MagLites and preferred by law enforcement officers in the field, whom I have actually stopped on several occasions and asked for their specific opinion on this subject. The first aid kit is a perfect place to store an extra bulb for each flashlight too. The smaller MagLite comes with a sheath which can be worn on your belt.

I recommend flashlights which use at least two batteries because they last longer in terms of number of hours of light. If you plan to store your flashlights for more than a month with no plan to use them, remove the batteries to prevent leakage and permanent damage.

Knives

The second best investment you can make in a hand tool is a knife. Unlike the multi-tool, there are hundreds of quality products to choose from. I prefer a larger fixed blade hunting knife made in U.S.A by Buck Knife. It suits my requirements as an all-purpose tool. I can cut cord, clean fish, and in an emergency even open canned food (although not recommended, you're supposed to have a can opener when camping!). Like your multi-tool, keep your knife clean, sharp, and rust free. A dull knife is far more dangerous than a sharp one.

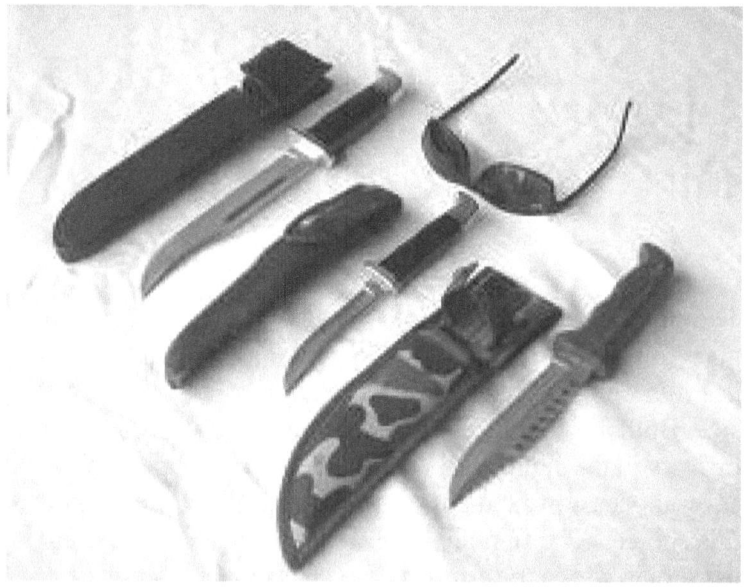

Multi-Tool

By far, the best investment I have ever made in a hand tool is the multi-tool. Don't buy a knock-off, I recommend the one made in U.S.A. by Leatherman, a company which specializes in manufacturing multi-tools. You'll pay $70.00 or $80.00, but it's worth every buck. I wear mine all of the time I'm in camp. Keep your multi-tool clean, sharp, rust free, and it will last a life time.

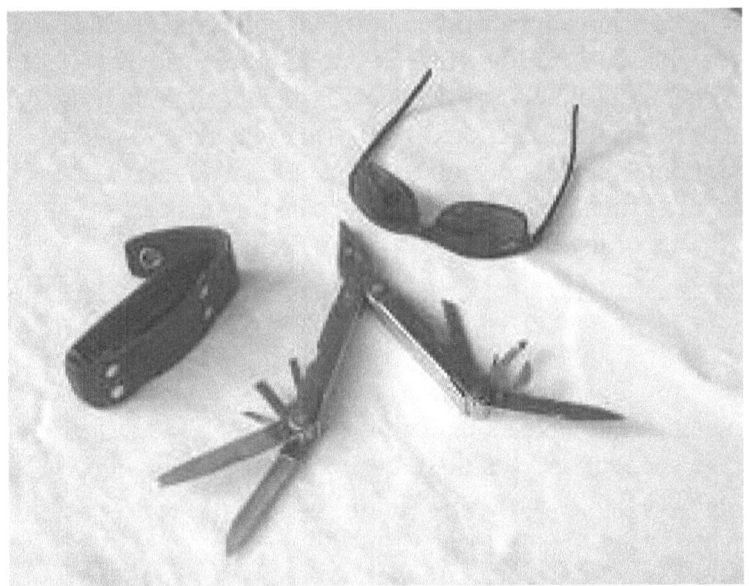

Summary, Equipment

In staying with the theme of keeping camping simple, I have detailed the minimal tool and equipment requirements necessary to ensure comfort and safety. However, I would like to offer a few more observations.

Beware, there are many gadgets waiting for your wallet. Gadgets which work great on TV and in Internet videos unfortunately don't work as well, if at all, in the field under real life scenarios. My favorite among these gadgets is something called a "pocket saw", which is nothing more than 18 inches of serrated wire with each end crimped to a key ring. I bought one once out of curiosity, and it snapped the first time I tried to use it. The camping toaster is another of my favorites.

I've never seen bread actually toasted over an open campfire using this gadget that looked like the picture on the box. Other gadgets, like "waterproof" containers for matches and table cloth clamps are optional. But, rather than spend money on these items, why not pack your matches in a freezer bag. And if you must use a table cloth, why not simply use rocks to anchor it?

I recommend staying away from tents, sleeping bags, and camping chairs that are specifically targeted at children (the kind decorated with cartoon characters and the like). Most often these items are of poor quality and will not achieve the goal of simplicity and comfort. And, you'll probably pay at least the same amount for these "toys" as you would for the real thing.

Another option for the camp stove is the type which uses unleaded fuel, sometimes called "white gas". White gas is a liquid fuel similar to gasoline used in vehicles. I have used this type of stove many times in the past. In fact years ago white gas stoves were your only option, there were no propane models such as the one I recommended earlier in this guide. One big disadvantage with gas stoves is having to pack a gas can. Gas cans often leak after opening, and you must be careful to pack the gas can such that it always stays upright. A funnel is required to fill the tank for the stove, and the stove tank must be pumped to pressurize it in order for the fuel to disperse to the burner of the stove. Depending on altitude and weather, getting a white gas stove lit can be a major headache.

Chapter 3 First Aid Kit

Build your own first aid kit. Buy a plastic fishing tackle box, the kind where two or three shelves unfold as you open it. Most of the stuff you need you probably already have around the house. Building your own first aid kit is much less expensive and the end result is far superior to the expensive store-bought kits. Also, a first aid kit doesn't always have to be synonymous with life threatening emergencies. Include such items as a sewing kit (the kind you get when staying at a hotel, for example), extra shoe laces, and safety pins. And it's a great place to store extra mantels for your gas lantern.

I have included a list of items I carry in my first aid kit later in this guide. I especially like those sample packets for antacids, sun screen, aspirin and so forth. They fit nicely into a tackle box, and you don't have to buy a whole bottle of whatever you have sample packs for. Your first aid kit can double for both camping trips and emergency preparedness, so be sure to inspect your kit regularly for expired medications and re-supply if necessary.

Whatever space you have left over in your tackle box/first aid kit should be filled with as much extra sterile gauze and elastic bandage in roll form as possible.

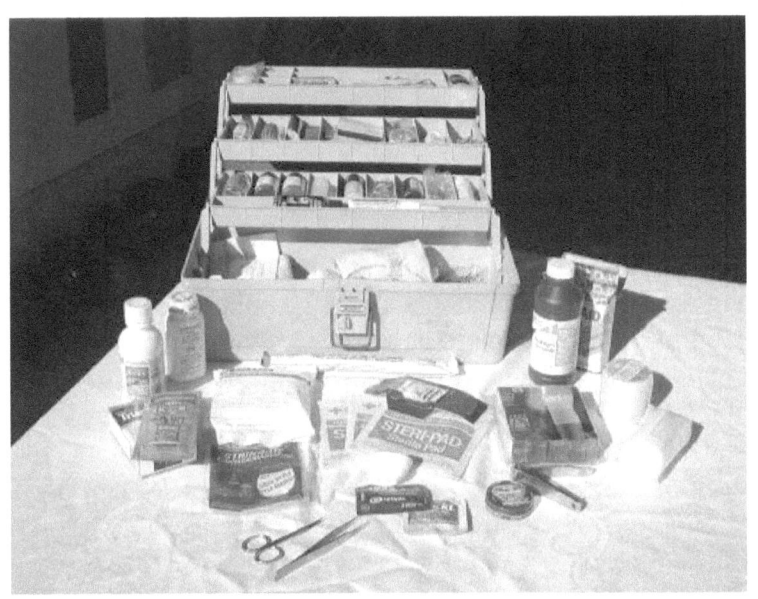

In my opinion, sterile gauze and elastic bandage are likely the two most important materials you'll need in an emergency. I also add items I wouldn't classify as first aid, but since the tackle box is a convenient place for storage I include the following items as well: toothbrushes, toothpaste, floss, shampoo, comb, insect repellent, whistle, matches, eyeglass repair kit, vinyl repair kit, and a small oil stone for sharpening knives.

Chapter 4 Packing and Unpacking

My goal for packing and ultimately loading all of my camping gear is to eliminate the need to tie anything down. Pack aerodynamically, you won't have to use a cargo net, and you'll save a lot of aggravation tying everything down. For example, pack umbrellas with the point facing towards the front of the vehicle. The same goes for collapsible camp chairs using a cover – pack them so the end that is not tied shut is facing forward. Rectangular shaped tubs which stack (like those shown below) are ideal for loading into the back of a pickup truck, SUV, or the trunk of a sedan. I pack soft bulky items such as sleeping bags and pads into larger duffle type bags for stuffing into the remaining spaces.

If I am taking the family for a week though, I have no choice but to tie off the duffle bags on top of heavier items. I use both tie downs and rope (See Appendix D for details on tie downs and knots). I don't care for cargo nets because they tend to get tangled which causes the whole loading process to take more time. Limit each camper to one small duffle bag (depending on the length of the trip), and check the bags as though you ARE airport security. I once caught my wife trying to smuggle an iron (never mind her excuse!).

Roof top cargo carriers with compartments are ideal for sedans and SUV's. As I mentioned before, I recommend the high-end hardware. It's expensive, but it will save you a lot of headaches in the long run. Plus, the expensive rigs can double as bike carriers. Soft bulky items such as sleeping bags and pads should be packed in the roof top carrier, while heavy items such as provisions and water jugs pack well in the trunk. If you go the less expensive route with just the crossbars, then you're likely going to have to secure everything with a cargo net.

If you have a sedan and simply don't have enough space for all your camping gear, consider a small utility trailer. The one I had was bought as a kit which I had to assemble. That worked out well because as I assembled the trailer, I reinforced the siding and added cleats for securing the cargo net. I also changed the wheels out to a larger size for better stability. One great advantage with a trailer is you can always have it packed and ready to go at a moments notice either for a quick trip to the lake, or in the event of an emergency.

I check my load, whether I in a pickup, SUV, or sedan before I get on the freeway and at all rest stops. As you travel the load will shift, so cinch up any loose tie downs and tighten up all of your knots when using rope. I've only lost items once from not being properly packed. Fortunately, it happened on the way home, and only a few pillows and blankets ended up as collateral damage.

Tip: Pack your vehicle in the reverse order that you will unpack upon arriving at your campsite. I pack my "kitchen" first, followed by storage bins, coolers, shade, and finally the firewood. The first item unloaded would then be the firewood, which I want to make sure is covered and stays dry upon arrival. I like to set up the shade as quickly as possible followed by tents and sleeping bags.

I recommend three knots in particular (See Appendix D for details on knots), the Bowline, Square Knot, and Taunt Line (also known as three "half hitches"). The Taunt Line is an easy knot to learn to tie. I use it to tie down everything from the heaviest loads (hauling appliances) to the guy lines on my camping shower. Just like a load shifts, the guy lines on camping equipment also shift as a result of wind, soft ground, or me tripping over them. It only takes a few seconds to tighten them all up. Another added bonus is unlike spaghetti knots, half-hitches are easy to untie.

Tip: Invest in decent rope, I prefer nylon. There is a huge difference between the qualities of $3.00 vs. $10.00 for fifty feet of cordage. I try not to have to cut smaller lengths than what I originally purchased. When I do, I melt the ends over an open flame until they bond. This prevents the cordage from unraveling and becoming basically useless.

Tip: One lesson I've learned is to pack your firewood in heavy gauge trash bags if there is any chance of rain. The firewood remains protected the rest of the way to your destination, and the extra added bonus is how much easier it is to unload a bag of firewood rather than a few pieces at a time once you arrive at your campsite.

Storage Containers

Since I have a pickup truck, it's much easier for me to pack larger containers for storage. I have a three drawer heavy gauge plastic cabinet serving primarily as my "kitchen". I also have several tubs with lids made of heavy plastic which are stackable and remarkably water resistant. I use one tub to pack all of canned and other non-perishable food, one for tents and poles, and another for inner tubes, pump, and Personal Flotation Devices (PFD's).

Smaller versions of a cabinet or tub shown here work well for packing in trunks or the back of SUV's. Any set of containers which stack are much easier to load, unload, and store. If you use containers with lids, make sure they attach securely, otherwise you'll have to tie them down with bungee cords or cordage.

All containers intended for storing provisions (food, toiletries, and other household items should have an effective method of securing the lids to keep the animals out. I have had raccoons actually lift unsecured lids from storage containers and losing a couple days worth of snacks.

Coolers

If your trip is scheduled to last several days, then you probably would like the ice in your coolers, which means the refrigerated provisions as well, to last until you break camp. Here are a few tips that should buy you an extra day without having to replenish your ice.

All of the drinks you plan to put in coolers should be pre-cooled, the colder, the better. Freeze all appropriate items ahead of time. Hot dogs, sandwich meats, even string cheese can be frozen, and will help conserve the ice (don't worry about the frozen stuff thawing, that'll happen on the way to your camp spot). Load up the coolers with ice the day before you plan on packing them so the coolers themselves will pre-cool. Take an extra cooler with only block ice to replenish other coolers later. And finally, on the morning of departure to your destination, drain all water and top off each cooler with as much ice as possible.

Chapter 5 Menu

When I take the kids, I get them to list items they want for each meal of the trip. I let them know they must submit their menus two or three weeks prior to the trip. I also let them know just because they wrote something down doesn't necessarily mean they're going to get it. As in cookies and candy - not going to happen (Okay, I'll give in to smores)! While I don't go on these trips either expecting, or expected to, provide gourmet meals, I also don't see it as an excuse for a lot of junk food. Obviously, fresh fruit and veggies are out of the question for longer trips, dried fruit (low in sugar, or sugar free), nuts, beef jerky, and string cheese are standard fare for snacking. As for drinks, I bring those small boxed juices, and plenty of bottled water.

In addition to what I bring as scheduled fare for the trip, I also bring plenty of additional canned foods, powdered milk, dry rice, dry beans, and other non-perishables. I want to be sure I have enough supplies to sustain everybody I am responsible for at least a week in case of an emergency.

Depending on the circumstances, I might prepare in advance items such as scrambled eggs, French toast, bacon, or sausage and then freeze them. Freezing steaks and pork chops (not cooked), for example, go well with canned vegetables and boxed mashed potatoes offering additional options.

There is often sort of a competition as to who can bring the most unusual snacking foods. Among the exotic fare are different varieties of stuffed green olives, pickled anything, obscure brands of salsa, Mexican cheeses, and even roasted seaweed have been some of the entries. So far, the delicacy pictured here is the winner!

Here are some suggestions for each meal:

Breakfast

Donuts, packaged (not a great promoter of health, but they last longer)

Granola bars
Hot chocolate
Instant oatmeal or other dry cereal
Pancakes (combine dry pancake mix with powdered milk)

Lunch

Sandwiches:

Hard salami
Tuna or chicken salad (use canned tuna, chicken)
Peanut butter and jelly
Potato Salad

Note: Don't forget bread for the sandwiches!

Dinner

Bar-B-Q baked beans, canned
Bean and cheese burritos
Chili, canned, straight or for chili dogs
Beef stew, canned

German potato salad, canned (goes great with the trout you'll be catching!)

Hot Dogs and buns (don't forget to bring hot dog sticks if you're camping in an area where you can't find your own!)

Macaroni and cheese
Soup, canned

Condiments

In addition to the obvious items like salt and pepper, I like to save those little packets of catsup, mustard, mayonnaise, and relish at every opportunity. Even though I use non-stick cookware while camping, I still like to have non-stick cooking spray and a little extra virgin olive oil on hand in case I catch a few trout. And, you can never go wrong by bringing all of your favorite hot sauces.

Snacks

Cheese and cracker packs

Fried pork rinds (I prefer spicy, and, this is a snack that's actually not too bad for you!)

Fruit cups (non-refrigerated)
Fruit rolls or dried fruit
Jerky; beef, turkey
Nuts
Olives

Pickled vegetables like ochre, cauliflower, and artichoke hearts

Popcorn
Pudding (non-refrigerated)
Roasted seaweed
String Cheese
Sunflower and pumpkin seeds
Tortilla chips, salsa, bean dip
Trail Mix

Note: Olives, pickles, and fruit cups are especially good when chilled.

Ice Tea

One of my favorite beverages is ice tea. Ice tea is perfect for camping because it's inexpensive and so easy to make. And, it's a great alternative to soda pop. Simply put four or five tea bags in plastic gallon of drinking water. Leave the strings on the tea bags such that when you cap the bottle, the strings are hanging on the outside. Set the gallon water bottle in the sun for a few hours.

When the tea has finished steeping, you can pull the tea bags out of the bottle by the strings. Add lemon and sweeten to taste. I like to put the bottle in the lake or river for an hour or so to chill, then serve on ice.

Coffee

I'd like to devote a small section here on the subject of brewing coffee on a camping trip. I have tried perhaps a dozen techniques for making decent coffee, and I finally found one that works great for me. And the coffee's not too bad either!

Several years ago while strolling through one of my favorite sporting goods stores, I happened across a small selection of coffee pots. I bought one made of steel and coated with porcelain, with the stem, basket, and basket cover made of aluminum. It cost about $15.00 and it's a percolator type coffee pot. I've found that even the already-ground-in-a-can store bought coffee tastes better!

Until I figured out a couple of little tricks, the first few pots were full of grinds, and my camp stove was full of coffee which overflowed the spout. The trick to minimizing grounds in the coffee is to simply place a paper coffee filter inside the basket. The trick to keep it from overflowing is to fill the pot up to about the bottom of the basket, and bring it not quite to boil, just hot enough to perk. Unlike your natural gas or electric range at home, your camp stove is using propane which burns much hotter. And you're probably higher in altitude which means paying more attention during the whole process. But it's well worth it. And, clean up is nothing more than rinsing the coffee pot after each use.

Drinking Water

I picked up a little tip from a fellow camper while on an outing some years ago. Up until then I never cared for bottled water other than gallon jugs if only for environmental concerns. But, the 16 ounce bottles are so convenient and as long as the little campers (and adult campers too!) are conditioned to finish the bottle and recycle, I no longer have an issue using these. The tip I learned is to add a lime slice right into the bottle along with any of the juice. You can use most any fruit, experiment and kick it up a notch!

Chapter 6 Tips and Tricks

Now that we've covered equipment and packing strategies in detail, let's review some of camping's "unwritten" rules and some simple techniques which will help prevent your camping experience from becoming a camping debacle.

I often half-seriously suggest to board members of my home owners association how they could save considerably on signage and memos if they simply post what is allowed versus what is not. Camping has its own set of rules and regulations. Just like the home owners association, they are mostly common sense courtesies intended to ensure all may enjoy the outdoors. Unlike a home owners association, camping has rules and regulations which are not necessarily clearly marked on a sign or posted on a kiosk, but must still be obeyed.

Rules for Little Campers, Newbie's, and Most Adults

Each camper must bring two pairs of footwear. One pair of sturdy boots for day use, and one pair of comfortable all purpose shoes for use around the campsite. When warm weather camping, everyone must bring one change of cold weather clothing and heavy coat. When cold weather camping, bring one change of warm weather clothing including a swim suit. You just never know.

I recall one trip I took to the infamous Mohave Desert in California in the month of August for the primary purpose of stargazing. My three companions were all highly educated, two of whom had PhD's. I noticed while packing there were only two sleeping bags and only a couple of heavy coats, one of each being mine, the other of which did not belong to the PhD's.

When I questioned them about where their sleeping bags and heavy coats were, they responded that because we are going to the desert in August it would be too hot, sleeping bags and coats would not be necessary. I warned them about how weather can change, even in the Mojave in August, but they're PhD's and I am not. I woke up the morning after the first full night out in the desert to find both PhD's walking vigorously about the immediate area, shivering, and trying to get warm. I never saw them again after that trip.

My most important rule is that all little campers must be within my FOV (Field-of-View) at all times unless accompanied by a competent guardian. Depending on age, each must carry a whistle, book of matches, and a pocket knife.

Wildlife

Take the time to research and educate everyone, including adults, and especially newbie's, about any poisonous plants, snakes, spiders, and scorpions.

RATTLESNAKES

Rattlesnakes may be found in this area. They are important members of the natural community. They will not attack, but if disturbed or cornered, they will defend themselves.
▶ Give them distance and respect.

Snakes come out of hibernation in springtime and when you should also be most vigilant. Be careful when gathering those rocks to use as anchors. I have turned up rocks on numerous occasions and found scorpions clinging underneath. Instruct the little campers never to put their hands in holes, brush, or anywhere they are not able to see in advance.

Poison Oak, Sumac, and Nettles are all poisonous plants indigenous to the areas I frequent most. I can tell you from personal experience Poison Oak is no picnic. And I've treated kids for Sumac and Nettles which are as painful as a bee sting. Don't hesitate to ask the Ranger, Camp Host, or Docent any questions you may have, read all signage, and take a stroll through the Visitor's Center.

Often times there is a kiosk located at campground and park entrances posting important, and interesting information about hiking trails, local plants and animals, warnings, and rules.

And, don't bother trying to skip any usage fees. I myself have never tried, but I've witnessed the boyfriend yelling at his girlfriend for talking him into it the night before, netting a $270.00 ticket in addition to the $20.00 fee the ranger collected on the spot.

Not all signs are for posting rules, fees, and dangers. Many, like the one below, point out areas of interest, inform you of local history, and describe local habitat. This sign was erected by the Bureau of Land Management describing the location of the local Post Office nearly a hundred years ago in the middle of California's Mojave Desert during a major gold strike.

Bear Country

Some campgrounds provide bear canisters and even bear proof steal lockers to store your provisions. The lockers are effective, but the canisters may only be as useful as how to much food and necessities one can hold and where it might be stored. Not likely a canister is going to do much good if a bear decides to use it as a soccer ball ending up down a 500 foot ravine. Most importantly though, never keep food or anything fragrant in your tent. This includes toothpaste, lip balm, gum, and even cosmetics. I also recommend not keeping such items in your vehicle as bears have been known to tear open car doors as though they were pop tops on a soda can. The most common method for food storage in bear country is to place all items in a container suitable for hanging from a tree. If you are unsure about what the rules are for preventing pillaging bears, ask a Forest Service Ranger, Camp Host, Docent, or an experienced neighbor. Never feed the bears, or any other wildlife for that matter.

Important tip: The best defense in the event of an attacking bear is to make sure you are with someone you can out run.

Just kidding!

Seriously, bears which may approach your campsite at a distance can be discouraged to leave by making a lot of noise. Yelling, slamming pots and pans together, having everyone look as large as possible (put on the heavy coats and ponchos) should do the trick. In the event of the worst case scenario, actually being attacked, it is widely accepted that rolling your body into a ball and playing dead is your best bet. You can't out run a bear, and bears are much better tree climbers than you are. I recommend avoiding areas all together where bears are known to frequent. Save the trips to bear country for late fall when they are beginning their hibernation period.

Tip: Even if you aren't in bear country, store all food items in your storage containers and secure the containers to keep out all the critters. I've lost a lot of my favorite snacks by forgetting to put them away for the night, or when I'm gone for a hike.

Plants

If possible, do some research before you leave for your trip. Shown here is what Poison Oak typically looks like during spring and early summer. There's an old saying: "*leaves of three, let them be*". Poison Oaks' signature three leaf clumps arc casily identifiable but there are many imitators. My general rule is "if you don't know what it is, leave it alone", and this applies to animals as well.

I am using Poison Oak as a specific example because I've had numerous personal experiences with it, and I've done a fair amount of research on the subject. Although the pictures shown here are colorful, Poison Oak can turn dry brown during the winter and can still pack a punch. Deer have been known to graze on Poison Oak when in this condition. Native American Indians would feed the smaller children the chutes of the plant to induce immunization.

Beware, this plant can appear as ground cover, grow as a shrubs many feet in height, and also thrives well by growing as a vine throughout other trees and bushes.

Although I know of no cure for Poison Oak, I have known of folks who swear by a product called Tecnu which is supposedly very effective (for Poison Ivy and Sumac as well) when used to wash affected areas. The next best option if you come in contact is to wash immediately, apply calamine lotion, and do your best not to scratch. The good news is, according to physicians I have interviewed on the subject, Poison Oak is not contagious. However, I would be careful about coming into contact with your dog if you suspect he's been rolling around in the brush.

And, although rare, people who are exceptionally allergic to Poison Oak may develop difficulty breathing if the toxin enters their respiratory tract. They should seek immediate emergency medical attention. Shown here is Poison Oak as it appears in towards the end of the summer season and into early fall:

Common symptoms from exposure to Poison Oak include a rash that can look intimidating, similar to clusters of mosquito bites. Typically, the rash will begin appearing anywhere from an hour to perhaps a day after contact. Beyond the initial outbreak, the rash may appear to "spread". Actually, the toxin doesn't spread; rather it just takes more time for certain areas of the skin to react depending on the length of contact and level of skin sensitivity.

I've briefly covered the consequences of coming into contact with some of the less desirable plants. I would like to take a moment and review a few more issues that fall into this category. Never, ever let anyone near any type of mushroom. Many mushrooms are poisonous, and most poisonous mushrooms result in death within a short period of time regardless of one's age, gender, or level of health. I instruct all newbie's on my trips about the dire consequences of so much as touching a poisonous mushroom. I remind all little campers never to kick mushrooms as the debris can result in contact.

Unless you are an experienced botanist, or have been formally trained about edible plants in the wild, I suggest never eating anything other than the provisions you brought for your outing. Berries growing on plants or shrubs are often pretty, easy to pick, and look like they may taste darn good. But, eating just a few may be enough to send a healthy adult to the emergency room.

Rather than scolding the little campers about approaching threatening plants, educate them (and in the process you'll learn something too) about the hazards of ingesting plants and wild fruits without knowing what they are. And be sure to approach the Park Ranger, Camp Host, or Docent to ask any questions you may have about the plants which share the environment with you.

Note: A Docent is someone who acts as a guide and is highly knowledgeable about the area you visit. Docents are usually volunteers and are always willing to answer any questions you might have.

Poison Oak Bouquets, and Humble Pie

I once lived in a small cabin in a rural area, near an
entrance to a Federal Conservancy. A Federal Conservancy
is a term used for land jointly controlled by the State,
USDA Forest Service, and the National Park Service.

Anyway, this is a true story. On one of my walks into the
park I noticed a couple of young ladies who had made
beautiful bouquets out of wild flowers nestled in a base of
bright red and green leaves from some vine type plant. (Uh,
you're not supposed to pick the wild flowers in the park,
but that's not my jurisdiction). I stopped them to
compliment on their creations. "Oh by the way, do you
have any idea what you are holding?" I asked. After
acknowledging they had no idea, I informed them they had
made the bases of their bouquets out of, you guessed it!
Poison Oak. I'm not sure they believed me; they walked
away without saying much. I recon they found out later
though.

Another time I noticed an elderly couple looking very
closely at some wild flowers along my driveway (nothing
more than 100 feet of dirt road). Out of concern for their
safety, I casually approached them and advised them to be
careful because of the Poison Oak nearby. The elderly
gentleman looked up at me and exclaimed "Young man, I
am a Professor Emeritus at the UCLA Department of
Ecology and Evolutional Biology, and I should think I
would know what I am doing by now!" I proceeded to
apologize and take a large bite of humble pie.

Campground Etiquette

Just like the neighborhood you live in, developed campgrounds have rules such as discharging of firearms not allowed, posted quiet hours, and the maximum number of campers and vehicles per campsite. These are simple common sense rules meant to benefit everyone by focusing on enjoying the outdoors.

Regrettably, there are going to be those who break the rules by staying up and blasting "music" all night long ruining the camping experience for everyone else. Always one bad apple. If you can, get a phone number for local law enforcement and don't hesitate to call to report delinquent or dangerous activity. Flag down the Camp Host or Forest Ranger to voice your concern.

You will likely meet people from many different backgrounds and skill levels, most of whom share a common fondness for being outdoors. Some may live at a campground due to unfortunate circumstances in their personal lives, while others have particular interests such as plants, animals, or perhaps just fishing. It's common sense to maintain at least a minimal level of vigilance. On one trip I took with a buddy of mine to a developed campground in the Cleveland National Forest near San Diego, California, we were approached by a young man with a five foot live snake perched on his shoulders around the back of his neck. As soon as I picked up on exactly what he had, I immediately ordered him well away from our site. Needless to say, I didn't wait to find out what his intentions were, I simply went into an instinctive mode and did what I thought was right.

I take my daughter, nieces, and nephews on many of these trips where I am the responsible adult, and in hindsight I may have overreacted. I am not a formally trained herpetologist so I had no way of knowing whether the snake posed a threat. However, like anything else, if you don't know what it is, leave it alone. I'm sure this young man was just a novice who got a little too enthusiastic with wanting to show off his prize.

Keep your campsite tidy. Tie off plastic trash bags to one of the legs of the canopy to make it easy for everyone to deposit trash. Dump your trash each evening into the campground dumpster so you don't wake up the next morning to trash scattered everywhere by the critters. Many campgrounds have specific receptacles for which to recycle your aluminum cans, glass, and plastic containers. Use them. Maintaining a clean campsite will help keep critters from getting into your food and it will put a smile on the Ranger's and Camp Host's faces.

Unless you are planning to camp primitive on public land I suggest you leave the following items at home:

All types of fireworks
Archery equipment
Sling shots
BB and Pellet guns
All firearms which discharge rim fire or center fire cartridges, BB's, and pellets

In addition to firearms using cartridges, many jurisdictions classify sling shots, bows and arrows, and BB and pellet guns as firearms. The same laws apply for these as well and are subject to the same penalties. I have even witnessed firearms and alcohol prohibition ordinances heavily enforced. I don't want to ruin your party; I am just recommending you pay attention to the rules.

Camping with Dogs

While I have never taken any of my dogs beyond a day hike in the local mountains, I do have considerable experience camping with dogs belonging to one or more fellow campers in my group. I leave my dog behind when camping as I do not want to risk injury or loss of my dog, either of which can happen in a blink of an eye. Many wilderness areas prohibit dogs. You must confirm what the rules are (such as leash requirements) before considering taking your dog on any camping trip. The primary concern by the authorities is the disruption of wildlife and other campers, and it's not necessarily the dog that is responsible, most of the time it is the owner.

Dogs require constant hydration particularly in the warmer months. Obviously, the larger the dog, the more water (and food) will be needed. Your dog should be tagged with appropriate identification or preferably micro-chipped as collars can get caught up in brush and tags can fall off. I've seen dogs on several occasions get spooked and take off into the forest. Fortunately, after hours and miles of searching they were ultimately found. I suggest dogs remain on a leash while in camp and overnight. Dogs off leash (if it is permitted) should be well trained to stay within a reasonable distance of their owner. Dogs should be trained to return to the owner on command if the dogs become distracted by any wild animals, poisonous plants, other dogs, and other campers. Dogs are going to know long before you do if there is a squirrel, rabbit, snake, or bear in your vicinity.

Dogs should be treated for resistance against fleas, ticks, and chiggers. Dogs are not immune to mosquitoes, consult your veterinarian about what to use as mosquito repellent on your dog. Your dog should be up to date on all vaccinations, especially rabies. Your dog should be groomed at the end of each day to eliminate any "hitchhikers" such as fleas and ticks.

The pads on dog's paws are generally not suitable to withstand prolonged contact with hot or coarse surfaces. I have seen paws literally shredded after a days hike over rough terrain. While "boots" for a dog sounds like a good idea, I doubt the dog will agree. It might be a good idea to bring extra gauze and tape and hopefully the bandaging, if necessary, will stay in place.

And finally, as part of the "Leave no Trace" directive, dog waste must be disposed of in the same manner as described for people in the section on personal hygiene when primitive camping, otherwise pick it up and put it in the campground trash receptacle.

The Lady Mountain Biker

As I have mentioned, you will no doubt meet people from all walks of life and varying demeanor. The more people who show consideration for others, the better the camping experience will be for everyone. For me, one ironic peculiarity about my journeys seems to stand out. I'm always presented with a situation whereby at least one individual needs some kind of attention. And it doesn't make much difference how far off the beaten path I go to try to gain the seclusion I desire, if only for a weekend.

Most of my experiences involve jumper cables and earlier in this guide I talked about the stranger with a snake wrapped around his neck approaching my camp. And yet another of my outings visiting the local mountains was no exception.

Note: Never approach a camp without announcing yourself and your intentions well before entering someone else's outdoor domain. Yup, just like in the old West, movies and all.

As it happened, I picked a beautiful campsite situated right next to an apparently popular trail head for mountain bikers. A lady on a mountain bike pulled up next to my spot and called out asking me if I new where the trail leading down the mountain ended up. I replied that I did not. She repeated the question again, and again I replied that I was not familiar with the biking trails. Then she asked me "Should I go down?"

What kind of a question is that? I'm not making this up! All I could think of was responding with "I wouldn't go on any trail unless I knew where it went". She repeated the same question, and I repeated the same response. Three times! After which I believe I heard something of a profanity directed at me as she was leaving. I did notice she was decked out in what appeared to be official mountain biking apparel, whatever that is, but what I really took note of was the only provision she had was a quart sized bottle presumable for water. I had no idea if she actually had water or anything else in the bottle. She wasn't wearing a backpack or waist pack so I assume she had no extra clothing and I doubt she had so much as a granola bar. At least she was wearing a helmet.

A half hour or so later she was back! She called out to me that she had located a kiosk with a map and now knew exactly where she was going. Well, I never read or heard anything in the news about anybody getting lost when I got home so I assume she made it. But as I have already stated, it never ceases to amaze me when people do get lost, and sometimes for good, many times only a couple miles from a major population center.

A different trip but same basic scenario. A couple of young men, perhaps in their early twenties, approached my camp and asked me, get this, "Can you spare some matches?" How does one go camping, or anywhere else for any reason without at least taking a book or two of matches?

Of course I gave them matches; in fact I gave them a box of stick matches hoping that might add some insurance for a quiet evening. As I handed them the matches I asked sarcastically if they had any plans to cross Death Valley next August without water. I don't think they got the message. My intention was not to be condescending, only to impress upon these young men the importance of preparedness.

One more short story for the road:

The Boulder Lady

I have mentioned you'll meet all kinds of folks when you go camping. The vast majority are amicable and are on the same journey you are – to seek peace and quiet while enjoying the natural surroundings. It's the vast minority that I seem to be blessed with having to interact with to some degree on many of my outings. I am always happy to assist anyone in need whether or not I am camping, but there are always those who will either take advantage of the situation or have nothing better to do than cross examine you as though it's your fault things didn't work out exactly as they had expected.

Not too long ago on one of our week long trips camping along the river at our favorite spot, I had yet another encounter with just such an individual. My buddy had gone back to camp to replenish ice and drinks while I stayed down at the beach soaking up a little vitamin D. I could hear some semblance of a voice hollering down from behind me, but I didn't pay attention because I couldn't understand what was being yelled over the sounds of the rushing river. And besides, I knew my buddy wouldn't even bother to yell anything under those circumstances. The hollering continued for several minutes when I finally got up and turned around to see what the commotion was all about. A rather large middle aged lady had been trying to get my attention now for about ten minutes. She kept yelling at me, I just waved and proceeded to climb all the way up the bank to see what she wanted.

She asked me if I was the camp host, and I told her I wasn't. Then she asked me "Why are all these boulders here?" Say what? I wasn't going to give a free lecture on the history of how the last ice age caused such natural erosion when it receded some 10,000 years ago. Then she shoved some brochure in my face and exclaimed "This is what it's supposed to look like, here!" All I could do was tell her I had nothing to do with the boulders or her brochure. At least I responded to her squawks. Apparently she and her husband (who hid behind her as best he could the entire time) had trampled over our camping spot without any regards for consideration of others. So when she approached my buddy and before she couple open up on him, he simply told her to leave now. I don't make this stuff up!

Chapter 7 Setting up Camp

Since I am the one who does most of the planning, preparation, and packing for an outing, it seems only fair that all of my campers pitch in with setting up camp. Even the littlest campers can unload the firewood, even if it's only a stick at a time. Assigning tasks teaches responsibility at an early age and encourages participation in the experience as a whole. One of my rules is no play until everything is setup. I know, because after play, I'm not going to get much cooperation with the work part.

The older kids, and newbie's, can learn to setup a tent, layout sleeping bags and pads, and setup chairs and tables. Naturally, my chair is the first to be setup immediately upon arrival where I then assume the role as supervisor. It's a tough job, directing all the setup activity from my post, cold drink in hand. Anyway, I wish that were the case!

Also, once on the road heading towards our destination, I encourage my campers not to speak about coming home until the last night of the trip.

Selecting a Spot for Your Tent

The most important strategic issue is where to setup the tent. Obviously, rocky terrain is out of the question, but since I prefer foam for use as sleeping pads, missing the clearing of a few small rocks isn't going to ruin a good night's rest. I do recommend taking a small rake which can make quick work of small rocks and other material as well as leveling out the spot.

First, I recommend against pitching the tent directly under large trees, particularly those which can drop sap onto your tent. Sap is almost impossible to remove, and it's just a mess in the long run when packing and unpacking a tent (or any equipment for that matter) covered with the stuff. Second, I recommend not setting up tents under large trees simply because falling branches can cause serious injury, or worse. Third, taller trees are more likely to get hit by lightning. Lastly, birds like trees and they don't care whether they are perched over your tent if you catch my drift.

Read the camp spot like a golfer reads a green before putting. You don't want to setup your tent at the bottom of a basin even if there is just a few inches difference in elevation. Even in a short downpour, an inch of water can accumulate in a matter of minutes soaking whatever's sitting in that basin. Now that you know to pick higher ground on which to setup your tent, read the terrain to see where any runoff might occur. I suggest using the heel of your boot and crease around tents and the campfire ring to direct any runoff around them. They don't have to be very wide or deep, just an inch or so should do it, any runoff will take care of the rest by default. The concept is not to try to block runoff; the goal is to divert the runoff around the tent. U.S. Forest Service personnel I have spoken to have no problems with creasing as it preserves the camping area for future use therefore discouraging more campsites and fire rings to be constructed. As part of the "Leave no Trace" doctrine, creases should be filled and groundcover restored as part of breaking camp.

If you're in an area subjected to wind gusts, I suggest selecting a spot behind a smaller tree, large brush, or boulder offering some shelter. If necessary, you can tie off where the tent poles intersect at the top to a small tree or shrub into the wind. Angling a corner of the tent into the wind can lessen some of the stress on the tent poles and tent walls. Leaving the flaps open also helps, in fact, leave the flaps open during hot days – but always keep the screens closed to prevent the creepy crawlies from entering.

Flash Floods

As long as we are on the subject, and since I do a lot of primitive camping, one of the acts of nature I am always on the look out for is any potential for flash flooding. There is a reason why flash floods are called what they are – the flooding can occur before you realize what is actually happening. Potential camping spots must be evaluated in anticipation of any possibility for floods. The cause is typically sudden heavy rainfall in a short period of time. However, you must realize it could be raining heavily dozens of miles up the river or dry canyon where you may not be aware of the potential for flooding. The rule is simple: always assume the possibility of flash flooding and select your campsite appropriately. A spot on or towards the peak of a hill or knoll would be a much better choice over a dry river bed.

Incidentally, localized flash flooding has also been known to be caused by the failure of a natural barrier upriver. The barrier could be a combination of boulders and fallen trees which have accumulated in one particular spot over many years resulting in a sort of natural dam. Even dens built by beavers have been known to burst, causing flooding downstream. We all know what happens when a dam gives way.

One experience I had was during a day picnic alongside a large creek. It was a warm, sunny day without a cloud in sight. I watched the kids playing along side the creek while sneaking a moment here and there to read. At one point I looked up from my book and noticed the creek had grown into a river and was about to make an island out our shoreline picnic spot! Within just a few of minutes, kids and picnic items were in the truck and we proceeded to move to higher ground. After an hour or so the river receded back to being a creek and we resumed our picnic. I never did find out what happened that afternoon, but I'll never forget how quickly the landscape had changed.

Firewood

I purchase firewood indigenous to, and bought locally in the area I plan to camp. Buying firewood discourages irresponsible campers from picking the forests clean of dead wood, live tree branches, and other plants. Also, bringing firewood from outside the area you are camping can introduce foreign plant or insect matter into the local environment and ultimately cause serious damage.

I usually get a mix, mostly hard wood which burns hotter and longer. But, I have to plan to make sure I also select wood which can be used for tinder and kindling. You'll need every advantage you can get if you have to start a campfire in the rain.

The firewood you purchase should be cut to length, preferably no more than two feet. And, unless you plan to split logs, I wouldn't get anything larger than five or six inches in diameter. Select an even mix of sizes; you'll want smaller sizes for starting your campfire each night, and a proportionate number of larger pieces as well. This obviously saves having to split and cut firewood at the campground which can be an enormous chore.

The cabin in the mountains I mentioned earlier in which I lived only had a wood burning stove for heat. I bought firewood by the cord. The cord was usually a mix of pine, oak, eucalyptus, and other varieties. Pine is easier to start, but burns quickly. Eucalyptus is difficult to start and even more difficult to cut and split, but burns long and hot. I recommend oak if you have a choice.

I don't recommend burning any treated wood such as scrap from a construction site, pallets, or furniture. Treated wood produce fumes which can be toxic, I wouldn't roast hot dogs or heat smoors over a campfire burning treated wood. The same applies for burning plastic cups, wrapping, and utensils.

The Campfire

Most developed campgrounds will include fire rings, or pits, and perhaps some type of grill. Once again, the shovel comes in very handy to dig out the fire pit.

Although I've used a number of methods to start campfires, such as flint and steel, and magnesium bars, I am on vacation. The theme is always simple and comfortable. So I use the tried and true fire starting method called lighter fluid. Yeah, it's cheating a bit, but I figure I've put in more than my fair share of time and effort over the years using other fire starting techniques. Before beginning to build your campfire, use your knife to shave off strips of wood which can be lit by a match. This is called tinder; a handful should do the trick. Using an ax or hatchet and split a dozen or so pieces about the size of a drinking straw, and maybe a half dozen pieces the size of a road flare.

Note: Did you know a dull knife, ax, or hatchet blade is actually much more dangerous than a sharp one? Tools with dull blades can "bounce" off the wood you are trying to cut causing you to lose control of the tool and increasing your risk for injury. There are many fine guides available showing you how to sharpen and maintain blades for any tool.

Set the ax or hatchet blade with the grain by hitting the wood with the blade while at the same time hitting the wood on a solid surface. Use just enough force to set the blade into the wood. Then you can lift the ax or hatchet with the piece of wood attached (without worrying about your other hand) and hit it against a solid surface. Using this technique precludes you from having to take a full swing of the ax or hatchet at a relatively small target.

The teepee method is the most effective way of starting a campfire and requires the least amount of work. If you take the time to set this up right, it will light with one match. Assuming the old ash in your campfire pit or grill is completely burned out, empty the ash into a trash bag and discard into a trash bin. The Ranger and Camp Host will be grateful to you.

Place paper items which would otherwise go to a landfill and use them as tinder at the bottom of the fire pit. Otherwise use the tinder you made as I described above. Begin building your teepee on top of the tinder using the kindling you split. Start with smaller, thinner pieces, followed by yet thicker, longer pieces.

What we're trying to accomplish by doing this, is to allow for enough oxygen to fuel the flame initially. In the picture above, I have purposely exaggerated a bit to illustrate the concept. This teepee would probably start with one match; however, you will want to use several more pieces of each size and more kindling to ensure an easy start. Once the kindling is going, gradually add increasingly larger pieces of wood. Challenge yourself and the other campers each night to see who can get the campfire going using just one match and no lighter fluid.

I have visited campgrounds with posted rules about how big of a campfire is allowed. It's usually something like three feet by three feet at the bottom, with flame no higher than about three feet. These dimensions are reasonable since you're probably going to want to conserve firewood to last the entire trip.

I strongly discourage throwing glass bottles and metal cans in the fire ring. They're not going to burn and it just causes additional work for whoever must clean it up. I've known a few folks who received citations in the mail for leaving their campfire ring full of cans and bottles.

I once watched, in quizzical amazement, as a couple of young men carefully built their teepee fire – using only three logs about three feet long and six or seven inches in diameter without the use of tinder and kindling. They actually expected to get it going! They eventually gave up so I walked over with some pieces of tinder and kindling and had it going in about half an hour. I have always been amazed at how difficult it can be to get a campfire going when you want it, yet campfires account for more than half of the cause of all wildfires in the U.S.

Sitting around the campfire with the kids might be my most favorite part of the trip. I like to point out the North Star, a few of the constellations, and even a planet or two. You can use a high power flashlight, similar to the one I described earlier, kind of like a pointing stick used by a teacher in a classroom. The best time for viewing the night sky is when there is no moon, and little local artificial light.

Depending on the age of the little campers, I like to tell scary stories around the campfire. There's the one about the Whitsitt Werewolf and another about Stumpy, the one legged man who goes out at night searching for a replacement leg. Little girls' or little boys' legs depending on your audience. And if there happens to be a cabin light off in the distance, point and exclaim: "Uh oh, Stumpy's light's on, he's out looking tonight!" And of course the ground snipes, those nasty part snake, part rat, animals with large fangs that only come out at night. Got to be careful of those! And don't forget the Camel Spiders.

Putting out the Campfire

I let the campfire burn down to hot coals without adding anymore wood when it's time to start thinking about lights out for the night. Dousing the coals with a five gallon bucket full of water should do the trick. If you expect any wind throughout the night, you may want to consider shoveling some sand (not organic ground cover) on top to keep embers from blowing and starting a forest fire. Move all camp chairs, tables, and anything else that could get blown into the fire pit at a safe distance. I've seen more than a few singed chairs the next morning because they were left too close to a fire which hadn't been put completely out.

Campfire Permits, Other Rules and Regulations

Campfire permits are generally required in undeveloped areas where wildfires pose extreme danger. Campfire permits are typically not required in developed campgrounds, however I suggest following the same guidelines for campfires in developed campgrounds as those in undeveloped areas.

Forest Service personnel will not issue a campfire permit
unless you have a bucket (at least a five gallon capacity),
shovel (a real shovel, not a gardening trowel), and water on
hand to fill the bucket (keep the bucket full at all times
once you have established camp). Be prepared to get a
lecture, listen, and don't blow it off.

They will make it crystal clear if you break any of the rules
such as having a campfire too close to a stream or river, or
if the campfire is left unattended, you will get a pricey
ticket. In the picture above, I have shown how I like to
neatly stack my firewood well away from the fire circle.
The shovel, 5 gallon water bucket (full), and fire
extinguisher (10 lb ABC) are always close at hand. Even
though the fire extinguisher, which I discussed in detail
earlier, is optional it will add an extra level of confidence
for you, the Ranger, and the Camp Host. You might even
be spared some of the lecture.

Always put out your campfire completely before leaving. If you're not willing to put your bare hand into the ash (and the Ranger will challenge you to do so), then it's not completely out. And you risk getting a healthy citation if it's not completely out.

Tip: if it appears the weather has a chance of turning wet, you might want to consider creasing around your campfire (just like you would crease around your tent) to keep any run off from putting out your campfire.

Be Prepared for Insects

I really only dislike two basic elements of nature which can ruin a camping trip: wind and insects.

Wind is simply miserable. If it's going to be too windy, I'll cancel the trip without hesitation. Insects are virtually unpredictable. I recommend, and never travel without, insect repellant and mosquito netting. Products containing DEET are generally preferred for repelling mosquitoes, ticks, and many types of flies. Insect repellant should only be necessary for use during early morning and the evening when most insects tend to make their presence known. Your tent should protect you at night assuming you keep the screens zippered shut at all times. Other types of insect repellent containing fragrances actually attract bugs.

Note: When unattended, always keep your tent zipped up to prevent mosquitoes, flies, and creepy crawlers out of your tent. Pay attention when entering and exiting your tent. I once put my hand down to where the screen was zipped closed only to find a scorpion sitting right there seemingly waiting to climb right in the tent with me for the night.

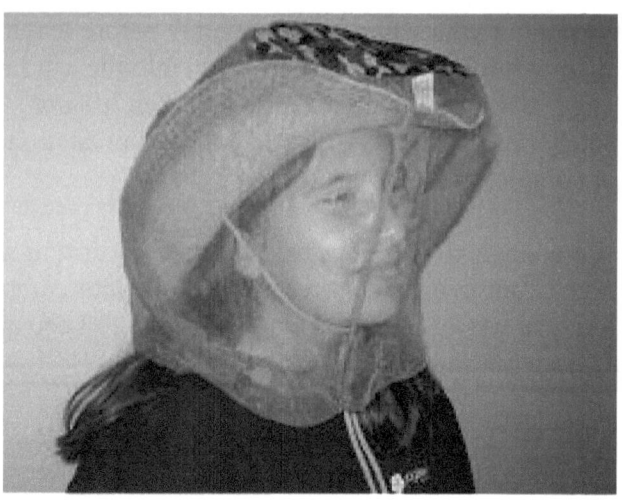

Mosquito netting, or better yet a head net, can be used to place over your head during the day. Secure it by wearing a wide brimmed hat. That'll keep you from performing the Australian Salute every five seconds by keeping biting bugs away from your face, particularly your eyes and ears But, don't forget to lift the head net before taking a drink of water or soda!

Another pest I am acutely aware of are Yellow Jackets. Yellow Jackets are carnivorous, in other words they go after anything made of meat or meat by-products and that includes you. The stronger the odor, for example an open can of tuna fish, the larger the swarm. Eating hot dogs roasted on a stick over a campfire can be challenging when one is swarmed by these aggressive pests. And getting bit by one is excruciatingly painful.

They seem to be worse at different times of the year, so I just plan on having to deal with them. You can purchase traps specifically for Yellow Jackets, but if you can't find them or you are otherwise without the traps, a neat trick is to make your own trap.

Take an empty plastic one gallon water container and cut a few "doors" on opposite sides about 3 or 4 inches from the bottom. Fill the container with a combination of water and a heavy dose of dish soap, ammonia, or bleach about half way to the "doors". Dangle a piece of beef jerky (or sandwich meat) on a string about 3 or 4 inches from the opening at the top of the container. The Yellow Jackets will be attracted to the bait, enter the doors, and ultimately become overwhelmed by the liquid. Place your traps out at the perimeter of you campsite because you don't want to get near them for quite awhile.

I have since found and field tested an extremely effective trap for Yellow Jackets. The trap is a bit expensive, about $15.00 for what amounts to a plastic enclosure with a top and bottom which unscrew allowing for inserting of the bait and emptying it for re-use. But, it's worth every penny. The key to this particular trap is the chemical attractant. Before attempting to use any type of trap, read all of the instructions very carefully. Misuse or make one mistake, will mean the difference between a wonderful trip and a miserable outing.

I am going to improve on the instructions a bit based on my experience. Start by using latex gloves on both hands when handling the attractant. The attractant is a liquid which comes in a small tube about the size of a stick of gum. Use scissors to very carefully snip the narrow end of the tube to apply the liquid to the cotton ball. The cotton ball is then mounted inside the trap. Once you break the tube of attractant, I recommend acting quickly. I also recommend having two adults deploy the trap; one to break the tube and apply the liquid to the cotton ball while the other secures the cotton ball (now bait) into the trap and places the trap at the perimeter of the campsite.

Meanwhile, the first adult disposes of both the piece of tube snipped off by scissors and the rest of the tube at the oppose ends of the campsite from where the trap is placed.

The first time I used this trap I had no idea how effective the attractant is. Within less than a minute the area where the pieces of tube laid on the ground were swarmed with Yellow Jackets. I had to use a shovel to move the pieces of tube to the other end of our campsite. Meanwhile, the trap had already begun to fill up with Yellow Jackets. I learned not to deploy these traps in your campsite; assemble them at the location you plan to place them.

Thirty to forty feet from your campsite should work fine, and you should need only one. This type of trap remains effective for up to two weeks or when it is completely full. If you get any attractant on clothing, immediately change out of the clothing. You may have to discard the clothing or even throw it in the campfire. Wash any parts of skin where the attractant has come in contact. You may have to use rubbing alcohol or even acetone (nail polish remover) to neutralize the effect of the attractant.

Day Hiking

"Be Prepared", the motto for the Boy Scouts of America, applies especially when going for a hike in the wilderness. Always wear appropriate footgear and take heavy coats. Matches, a map, compass, and a whistle can easily be placed in a coat pocket, so there is no excuse for being lazy. Better yet, I recommend one of those day packs, similar to what kids use for carrying books to school. A day pack can also accommodate lunches, snacks, a camera, and binoculars. You may want to consider using 2 way radios for communicating with "base camp" just in case.

The most important provision is water. Water in plastic bottles should work okay when carried in a day pack, but store-bought packaged plastic water bottles are flimsy. If you drop the pack, you may lose your water. I recommend aluminum water bottles. They are far more durable and designed to withstand a fall unless you happen to be on the rim of the Grand Canyon when you drop one. I still have a U.S. Army issue aluminum canteen I used in the Scouts. I can easily slide the canvass holder onto my belt, and the canteen is secured into the holder by a flap with a couple of snaps. You can find these at military surplus stores.

Not enough can be emphasized about hiking out of view of your campsite. I have read many stories over the years about lost hikers, some found within just a couple of miles of a major city such as Los Angeles, California. When folks tell me it's impossible to get lost anymore because of GPS technology, I remind them the Titanic was thought to be unsinkable. GPS may be overkill for the average day hike, it all depends on whether you are taking a marked trail (highly recommended), or plan to hike cross country.

Altitude, Acclimate, Hydrate, Pace

If there is any concern about your physical conditioning particularly in higher altitudes, consult a physician. If you are unaccustomed to higher altitudes, you may need time to adjust, or acclimate. Symptoms of altitude sickness include headache, nausea, and hyperventilation. When any of the campgrounds on my trips exceed 5,000 feet, I spend the first night and the next day acclimating to the altitude before taking any day hikes or engaging other excessive physical activity. For me, adjusting to higher altitudes actually takes several days before the downside affects are mostly gone. I never have conquered hyperventilating though!

This brings me to another topic: pace. I believe in eating when hungry, resting when tired, sleeping when my brain tells me it's time, and acknowledge the necessary physical attributes when the mind and body are ready. In other words, everyone in your party is likely going to have a different pace during a hike. I'm not going to get technical about establishing a unified pace, we're not in the military, we are doing this to enjoy!

So, what does all this mean? Planning ahead is great and always advised. But most of the time, at least for me, plans turn out to be dynamic (always changing) due to factors such as weather and other unforeseeable events. For this reason I plan on a daily basis what our day hiking goal might be. In addition, I also design as many backup plans as the map and surrounding area has to offer. In this manner, if I or anyone in my party becomes fatigued or exhausted, we can simply pull off the trail, rest, or return to camp. There is always tomorrow to reach that stream or lake.

Maintaining hydration is a top level priority at all times day and night. Dehydration by itself is dangerous; however dehydration combined with heat exhaustion, sun stroke, over exertion, and/or other potentially damaging elements can result in extremely high blood pressure, liver failure, and ultimately fatal consequences. The symptoms are similar in nature as already described for altitude sickness but are likely to be much more severe. Obviously, the trick is to avoid cause in the first place. However, I have seen cases where the symptoms were either overlooked or allowed to continue mostly due to simple unawareness.

I can tell you from personal experience that it's not difficult to get that "runner's high" feeling from a great day's hike only to become bedridden for a day or two – or worse. Know your limitations (which is why I recommend starting out with shorter trips and working you way up), stay hydrated, avoid too much sun and heat exposure, and rest at regular intervals.

Map and Compass

In my backpacking days before GPS became available and affordable, I did quite a bit of cross country hiking in the Sierra Nevada Mountains of California and other areas in the Northwest with topographic maps and a compass. USGS topographic maps by quadrangle and a compass with a dial to set a course was high tech at the time. And, one needed to know how to use them.

Actually it's easy and should still be part of any hiker's standard equipment in case the GPS unit fails. Oh, by the way, one of my tricks for preserving each of my USGS topographic maps is to laminate them between two sheets of clear shelf paper. If the map should land in a creek, it will not disintegrate.

For purposes of describing the basics of reading a topographic map, I have broken out each section pertaining to my discussion from the Mineral King quadrangle into separate images. Topographic maps are about 30 inches by 24 inches, making it unfeasible to include an entire map in one image in this guide.

All USGS topographic maps have an angle illustration measured in degrees located along the top or bottom portion of the map (shown a couple pages down). The angle shows the offset in degrees between magnetic North and true North for that particular region. Lay the map on a level surface, line up the map such that the angle indicating magnetic North is in the same direction of the compass needle.

Calibrate the compass for your cross country route by rotating the compass platform to point as close as possible to the feature you wish to travel to on the map: a pass, a lake, or perhaps an intersection of major trails. If you can visually see your destination, such as a lake from the pass you just climbed, confirm your compass setting matches the lake you can see with the lake on the map. Do not change the setting or otherwise tamper with the compass housing until you have reached your destination. Pictured here is my original Pathfinder compass:

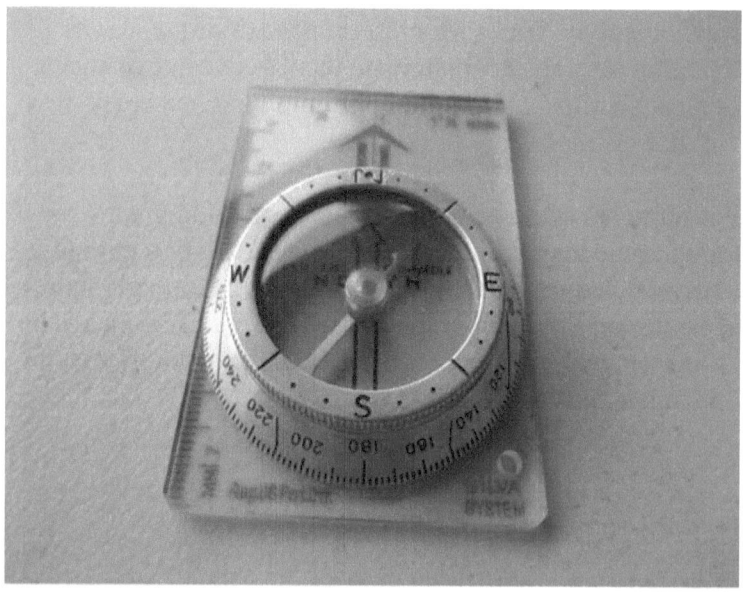

While hiking, periodically check your heading by allowing the compass needle to settle (pointing to magnetic North), line up the compass such that the needle is aligned with the etching of the arrow inside the compass housing and confirm you are traveling in the direction to which the compass platform is pointing. Depending on the terrain, it is unlikely your hike to your destination will be a straight line. Use other land marks to maintain a visual aspect of your approximate location and compare these features to the topographic map. The compass course is already set, all that needs to be done to insure travel in the right direction is to view the compass regularly. The compass needle will always point to magnetic North, and as a result, continue to travel in the direction the compass platform is pointed.

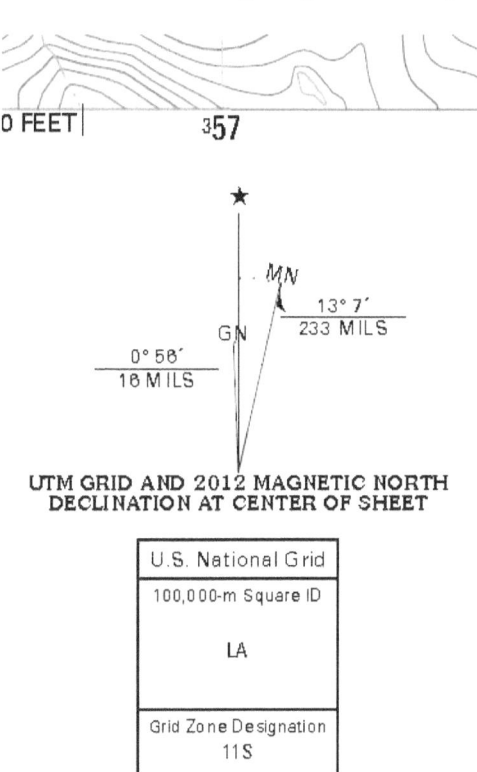

In addition to providing navigational assistance, topographic maps provide the same information as roadmaps such as those published by the Automobile Association of America including, scale, roads, waterways, mountain peaks, and trails:

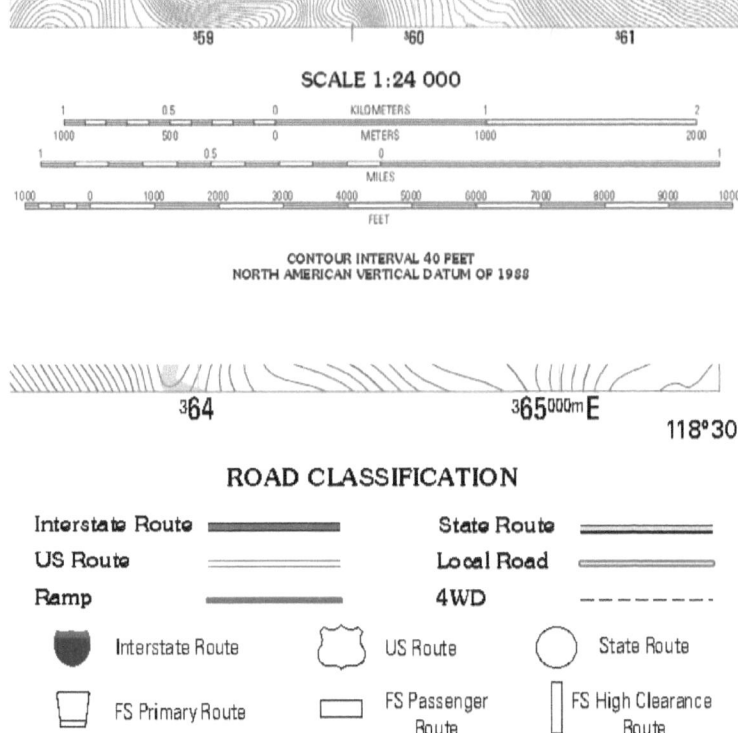

SCALE 1:24 000

CONTOUR INTERVAL 40 FEET
NORTH AMERICAN VERTICAL DATUM OF 1988

118°30'

ROAD CLASSIFICATION

Interstate Route		State Route	
US Route		Local Road	
Ramp		4WD	

Interstate Route   US Route   State Route

FS Primary Route   FS Passenger Route   FS High Clearance Route

Check with local Forest Service unit
for current travel conditions and restrictions.

MINERAL KING, CA

A topographic map consists of an area called a quadrangle and is measured in minutes. Here, I am using is a 7.5 minute quadrangle map which covers approximately 50 to 70 square miles. And, it's not uncommon to carry more than one map as you could travel over the boundary of a quadrangle. As part of the legend, a topographic map includes a visual tool showing the approximate location within the state and the surrounding quadrangles:

62   ³63

CALIFORNIA

QUADRANGLE LOCATION

Lodgepole	Triple Divide Peak	Mount Kaweah
Silver City	Mineral King	Chagoopa Falls
Moses Mountain	Quinn Peak	Kern Lake

ADJOINING 7.5' QUADRANGLES

123

Learn to read the contours on the topographic map and you will be able to accurately predict changes in elevation in advance during your hike. The next couple of pages are sections of the topographic map I used on my Big 5 Lakes backpacking trip. I had to break these sections out and rotate them so the detail of the trails, contours and other features could be seen.

The first part of my trip begins at the Mineral King trailhead located in the lower left hand corner of the first map section. My goal for the first night is Spring Lake which appears at the upper right corner of the first map section. I have annotated the trail using a light pencil tool for easier reference. You can see the first part of the climb out of the valley consists of perhaps a half dozen switch backs. Note the contours are much closer together indicating a much steeper ascent. The trail flattens out for a bit until reaching Monarch Lakes which is where I had lunch and a good rest. Look ahead and you will see why!

The next part of the hike includes at least a dozen switchbacks heading up to Glacier Pass. Once again, the contours are close together. Almost at the top of Glacier Pass you see the trail taking a hard right towards Sawtooth Pass, but that's way out of the way to get to Spring Lake. And, there is no established trail from that point to Spring Lake. Since Glacier Pass is a significant landmark and it's only another hour or so climb, I picked contours to hike along which were not too steep to reach the top. From my vantage point at the top of the pass, Spring Lake was in sight and first night's camp is only a couple hours of easy hiking away.

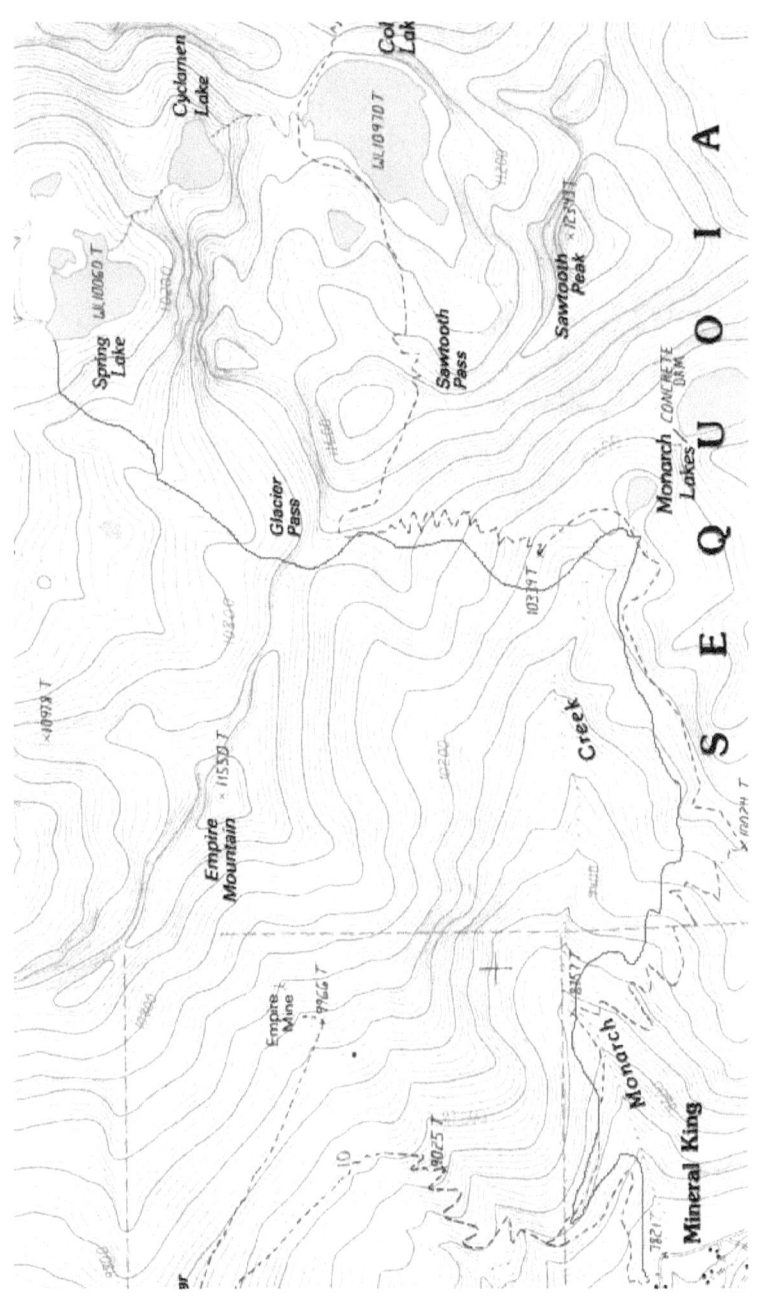

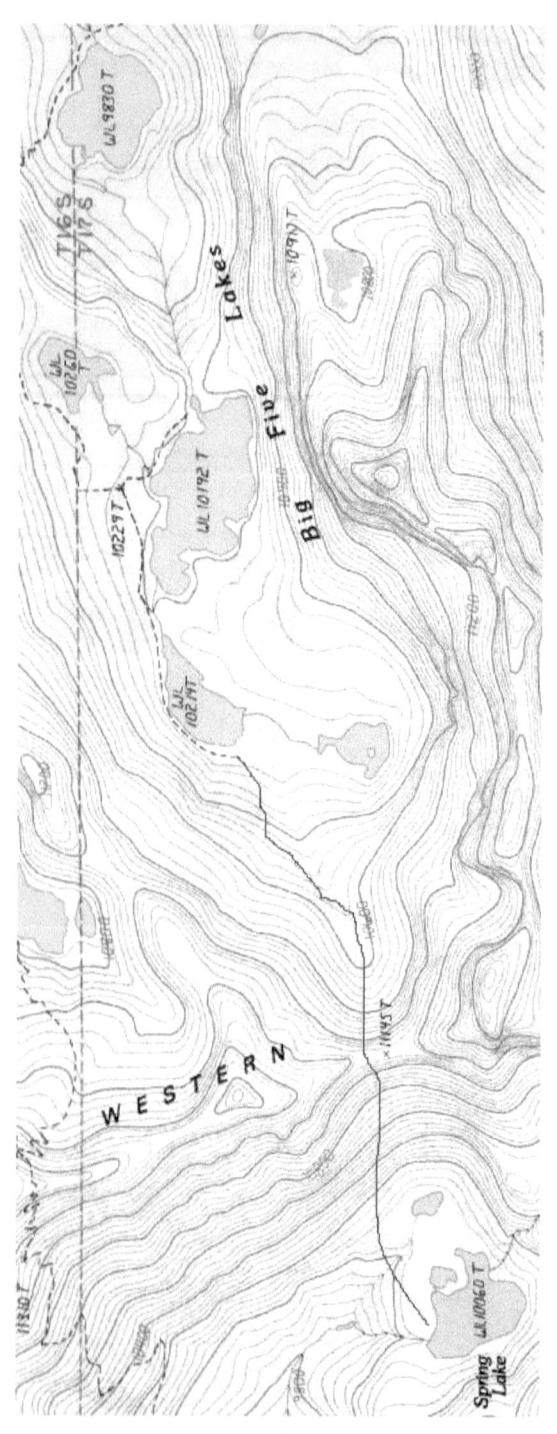

126

The next leg of the trip was climbing the next pass to get to my destination, The Big Five Lakes. The second map section shows Spring Lake in the lower left corner. My destination, The Big Five Lakes, is seen in the upper right of the second map section. Again, there is no established trail; however it was easy to follow where others had already compacted a path to the base of the pass. The contours on the topographic map show a very steep ascent, and indeed it is. The path disappeared half way up to the summit but considerate backpackers had left ducks (usually three or four larger rocks stacked off the side of the "trail") to show the way. A few times I had to use my hands to grab whatever solid rock I could find to pull myself up the pass. The view from the top was nothing short of awesome. Spring Lake was behind me and the Big Five Lakes ahead, an easy hour's walk.

Tip: without using a topographic map, set a compass course by lining up the compass housing to magnetic north, and then rotate the compass platform to a visible landmark in your neighborhood. While taking your evening stroll through your neighborhood, check the heading. Even though you won't likely be walking in the right direction, you will be able to visualize navigating by compass. Learning navigation by compass in your own neighborhood prepares you before venturing out into the backcountry.

Fun with Constellations

While this topic might appear to be out of place right after discussing the basics of navigation by map and compass, it turns out that people have been navigating by the stars much longer than by compass. Depending on the source, the first practical compass used for navigation wasn't invented until around the thirteenth century.

The discovery of the navigational properties of the North Star (Polaris) occurred about 1,000 years prior (again, depending on the source).

The Big Dipper is perhaps the most well known of all constellations. The Big Dipper is shaped like a ladle, hence its name. It is one of the larger features in the night sky and is easily recognizable. The following image showing the Big Dipper has been rotated to fit such that the detail can be seen in this guide:

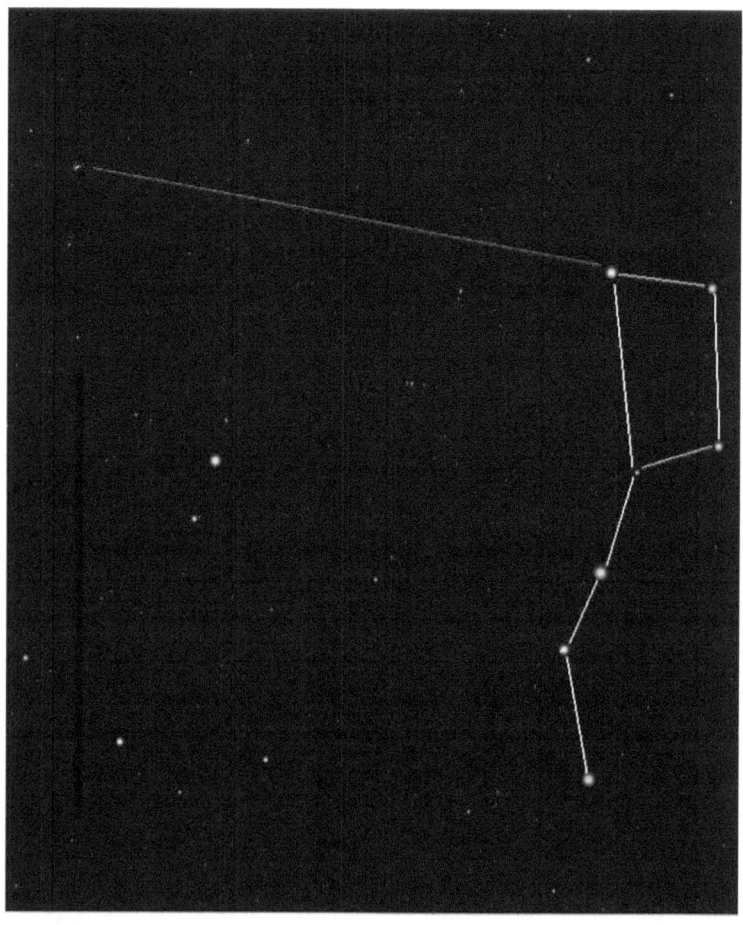

The orientation in the night sky may be different depending on where you are viewing and at what time of the night. The Big Dipper can always be found (assuming you have enough horizon) as it "rotates" around the North Star which is always in the same location. Upon locating the Big Dipper, note the far edge of the ladle.

Locate the North Star by measuring with your eyes (or use a finger) about 4.5 lengths of the ladle's far edge from the star on top of the ladle's edge in almost a straight line. The North Star is comparatively dim to other stars, but there are none more visible to the eye in that part of the sky. The North Star is also the outer most star of the handle of the Little Dipper. Have fun looking for and identifying dozens of other constellations!

Tip: use a flashlight with a bright narrow beam like a teacher uses a pointer to the blackboard to highlight features in the night sky so others can follow along.

The North Star can be used as a navigational tool on land by aligning a couple of stakes set into the ground. Set a longer stake first, and set a shorter stake behind such that the tops of the two stakes line up with the North Star. In the morning, you can line up the topographic map's true North angle to your stakes and see how close you are by comparing it to your compass.

Clearly, navigating by Polaris alone is not the best strategy; rather I'm discussing the concept for entertainment and informational purposes. Although, one never knows when it could come in handy!

Careful with Water

I mentioned earlier about living in a small cabin in a rural area near an entrance to a Federal Conservancy. The cabin was situated along a creek which was dry except during the rainy season. In springtime, when the weather was warm and the creek was flowing, it was a popular area for families to congregate and picnic. The kids had fun running and playing in the water, if not to keep cool.

Trouble was, and I wasn't about to crash anyone's picnic, all of the homes in those mountains had septic systems. And every time there was significant rain, most of those systems would overflow. Into the creek. Where the kids were playing. And I knew it because of the distinct odor following the water down the canyon. I don't know to this day if anybody ever got sick, but I never allowed any of my guests near that water.

The probability of anybody getting sick from swimming in the water at your campground is minimal. The chances of high concentrations of pathogens, or disease causing bacteria, decrease the farther away you get from populated areas. Because animals are also a source of pathogens, there is never a %100 guarantee of pure water.

The solution for avoiding getting sick is simply not to drink the water from any source other than tap or your own bottled water. Most developed campgrounds have tap water suitable for drinking. Although on a couple of occasions I have seen posted warnings when even the slightest concern with the water was suspect. I recommend using the bottled water you brought for the trip exclusively for drinking, and use tap water for cooking where you can bring the water to a boil for several minutes.

While out of the scope of this guide, if you think you must use water purification tablets or portable filtration systems, then you probably shouldn't be camping in the area in the first place.

Snow, Ice, and Freezing Conditions

Although snow, ice, and otherwise freezing conditions are outside of the range of conditions specified at the beginning of this guide, I have also made the point to always prepare for the unexpected. I have experienced moderate snow conditions on many occasions, most of which were unseasonable and certainly not expected. I have learned if there is any possibility of snow on any outing, I upgrade to a tent rated for all seasons and down sleeping bags (described in the "Sleeping Bag" section of this guide). Heavy coats (down insulated) are, for all intents and purposes required, as are heavy gloves, boots, leggings, and head gear.

The tents described in the "Tent" section of this guide are not rated for all seasons. Only an inch or two of snow or a little ice will cause these tents to collapse and may damage them beyond repair. It's not likely anyone will get hurt, but a severely damaged tent in freezing conditions does not fit into the comfortable camping theme of this guide. The only way to keep the tent from collapsing under the weight of any accumulation of snow is to periodically clear it off.

If you have portable shade such as the collapsible type described in the "Shade" section of this guide, or any umbrellas, you will have to periodically clear the snow and ice from them as well. It only takes an inch or so of snow or a thin sheet of ice to completely destroy a collapsible shade. The only remedy is to pull the cover of the shade off of the frame before retiring for the night.

Freezing weather presents more challenges, mostly when you try to use gadget items like fire starter tools and white gas stoves. Most of the equipment I have described in this guide will function properly in less than fair weather assuming key components have been reasonably maintained.

Water Safety

Many of my summer trips are planned specifically (and carefully) for spending time at a lake or river. One summer in particular presented me with a few more challenges than usual as the snowpack in California's Sierra Nevada Mountains approached nearly 200% of the annual average. Though there are always drowning incidents ever year, unfortunately California suffered a record number of deaths due to drowning during that spring and summer. Lack, or more likely a complete absence of common sense played a huge role that year.

One river in particular claimed the lives of seventeen people between the months of April and July, and all were preventable. The most notable event occurred in April when the river was at its peak flow producing class five rapids in virtually every area easily accessible by simply parking on the side of the road and walking 100 feet to the river bank. Two men about twenty years old attempted to ride a raft (the type purchased at the drug store normally for use by children in a swimming pool) without wearing Personal Floatation Devices (PFD's, also known as life vests). To top it off, neither of the young men knew how to swim.

The bodies were finally found two weeks later. On another occasion, a life was lost when an enthusiastic angler ventured into the river about knee deep and was immediately swept away. They didn't find him for several days. Yet another young man succumbed to the river after consuming alcohol, aka "liquid courage". I won't detail the other thirteen casualties; I think you get the picture.

Common sense dictates at very least asking locals about water conditions. I learned many years ago the local store near my favorite river side camping spot simply puts all of their floatation toys away when the river is running too high. Their motive may not be so much as looking out for potential customer's health and well being as a potential lawsuit if anyone were to get hurt on a toy purchased at their store. Consulting Forest Service personnel, law enforcement officers, or professional rafters and kayakers are also excellent sources of information.

Earlier in this guide I described flash flooding in considerable detail. Whether you're in the middle of the desert or along a mountain creek, flash floods must be taken into consideration year round. You likely cannot see severe storms high in the mountains fifty miles away which are capable of causing a river to rise dramatically. So much so, that in only a couple of hours the increase in flow may become too dangerous to enter the water.

One of the stupidest things I can think of when it comes to water safety is the floatation toys some people use. I have seen an eight foot tall inflatable swan with two guys attempting to ride the rapids mounted like they were on a horse. The river was at a safe level, but what's the point?

The swan "floatie" lasted about 300 feet before it popped and shriveled into a useless pile of vinyl. Then there are the cheap inflatable canoes that don't last the first run because they can't be steered and ultimately get sliced up by brush or sharp rock.

Now to my all time favorite example of zero common sense – water wings. These are absolutely the dumbest floatation "device" in existence. I can't believe people put these things on their toddlers at the community pool let alone on a floatie running class 3 or better rapids. Water wings should be outlawed. I had one experience where a mother briefly took her eyes off her toddler wearing water wings in the pool. I happened to catch the toddler out of the corner of my eye slipping out of the water wings and sinking like a lead weight. Fortunately, the child was only ten or fifteen feet away from me and I was able to get to her in just a couple seconds. The lesson here is that things happen very fast, and whatever situation or environment you're in, you must remain vigilant.

In my opinion, the ideal floatation device for "tubing" down a river or floating around in a lake, is well, an inner tube. Inner tubes can be found at many tire stores, particularly those that specialize in truck tires. Inner tubes are extremely durable (guess what, they're designed to stick inside of a truck tire, and trucks typically haul twenty tons or more at fifty five miles an hour, for thousands of miles). My second choice is the River Rat which is made of a heavy duty vinyl material and has a second separate chamber which should also be inflated inside the tube for added safety. I have never had an issue with either type.

Coast Guard approved Personal Floatation Devices should be worn depending on conditions of the river or lake. I don't want to sound like a party pooper, but I do agree that towards the end of the summer the river is going to be more like a creek and it's probably not necessary to wear a PFD. When tubing in a river, I observe four basic rules:

1) Never tie tubes or riders together in any way. If the rider falls in and gets tangled in a bunch of rope, that could mean serious trouble.

2) Ride the tube feet first. I would rather hit a rock with my feet than my head (consider wearing a bicycle helmet).

3) Always wear a Personal Floatation Device if conditions are appropriate.

4) Riders must know how to swim well enough to get to shore.

I have used the river scenario as the example for discussing water safety. However, much of my discussion applies to lakes as well. The greatest danger swimming in a lake is, unlike a swimming pool, the water is often murky with only inches of visibility. If the incident where I grabbed the toddler in the swimming pool instead happened in a zero visibility lake, it could have taken minutes to find her even as close as a few feet. The outcome of such an event could have been very different.

Just like storms high in the mountains can cause flash flooding, storms can cause conditions in larger lakes such that small boats will capsize and people drown. Camping at a lake offers you the benefit of viewing a large horizon allowing you to see potential weather issues as they form. Rivers, based on my experience, don't usually give you that advantage as you are often situated in a canyon limiting your horizon.

Personal Hygiene

I'm guessing the least pleasant, well let's face it, the most unpleasant aspect of tent camping are the restroom accommodations. This is probably the most significant issue that discourages people from tent camping in the first place. I have a few tips on how to deal with this subject.

Most of the difficulties I've had to overcome was having to educate the little campers. Through trial and error, I found instead of trying to encourage the little ones into an outhouse on their first few trips, I brought just the seat part of the old training potty. The seat could be set up on a few rocks behind a bush with mom right there to help. This technique ultimately paid dividends later when I could take the kids primitive camping.

Outhouses can be revolting to most. When the subject arises from a reluctant camper, I respond with questions as to what the pioneers must have done on their long journeys across the country in covered wagons. Did they carry restrooms with them? I think not. Did they build an outhouse every time they stopped for the night? I doubt it. Well then, I explain, having an outhouse would have been a luxury for the pioneers. I leave it up to the reluctant camper to figure out exactly how this situation was ultimately resolved by those pioneers. Add a few basic pointers like "don't look down", and that ought to do the trick.

Outhouses vary in terms of comfort level. Developed fee campgrounds with a camp host generally have accommodations which are well lit (during the day by sunroofs), well vented, and are kept relatively clean. Developed fee campgrounds without a camp host means the accommodations will typically not get as much attention but may still be tolerable.

Another way to gauge the quality of the accommodations is whether the campground is operated by a private company which leases from the Forest Service. Privately managed campgrounds tend to much better maintained than those overseen by the USFS.

Regardless of the type of camping trip or where my destination lies, I never leave home without at least one roll of TP per person, per about two days. Even though most developed fee campgrounds provide TP, the rolls are often times mounted on a steel bar. At best, you'll get only one sheet at a time. I just use my own roll to avoid this bit of frustration.

Although a bit more than I need, I have seen folks hang air fresheners and fly strips to improve the ambiance. Closing the lid and the door behind you will help keep flies and other critters out of the outhouse. By all means, use seat covers. Honestly though, I have never seen or read about any evidence whereby you can contract any disease from an outhouse seat.

I am sure that's not good enough to convince the germaphobes, but I am more concerned with whether the outhouse door locks securely, and whether the little campers will have any problems securing the door and be able to open it as well. A general rule for visits to the outhouse by the little campers, regardless of age, is they must go in groups. Otherwise, an adult must accompany any child. Unfortunately, you must be vigilant even at the remotest of campgrounds. One more rule I make very clear to all the little campers is that nobody is allowed to bother anybody in anyway when visiting the outhouse.

Primitive camping offers fewer alternatives. The portable shower with a portable potty can double as an outhouse. My preference is to just go about my business like a Neanderthal, but maybe with a portable potty and the disposable bag for a little added comfort.

I'm not going to argue the "pack out what you pack in" politics pertaining to this subject when camping primitive. Packing out human byproducts is not feasible and it is not safe. Although two to three hundred feet from any water source, campsite, or trail is generally acceptable to do your "business", I'm quite a bit more reserved. My acceptable distance is closer to a quarter mile and well out of sight (watch out for signs an area has been used recently). Dig a hole eight to ten inches deep. Fill it back up when done and lay a good sized rock or two on top, otherwise leave the immediate area just as you found it. Use biodegradable tissue. That's all there is to it.

Cleaning cooking gear, laundry, and bathing should be done without risking contamination of any fresh water source. Discard and strain all dirty dish, laundry, and bath water at least two to three hundred feet from any water source, campsite, or trail.

Ladies, This is Just For You

Obviously, scheduling your trip around "that time of the month" is the best possible option. If that is out of the question, or perhaps you need to prepare for a "just in case" situation, then there are several options to choose from, and of course, I am really not in much of a position to make any recommendations with regards to your choice of comfort or convenience, but at least I will give a go. Research, while arguable by some factions, has shown that some bears are attracted to used tampons and pads which are why care in transport or disposal is important. Black and brown bears of the Northwest are far less likely to have any interest, while grizzlies in other parts of the country will dine on such leftovers.

Non-biodegradable tampons may be convenient; however the "pack out what you pack in" rule applies here. Used non-biodegradable tampons should be double packaged in plastic zipper bags and hung similarly to a bear bag to keep animals at bay. Biodegradable pads may be disposed in the same way as bath tissue or they may be burned so long as the fire is very hot. Yet another option is to reuse a cloth instead of a pad which can be washed. Cups may also be an option as they can also be cleaned and reused. In either case, discarding the used water must be done in the same manner as the water after cleaning cooking gear or washing clothes. Although I expect to get criticism from suggesting these methods, my research and experience shows these are all acceptable methods.

"I am master of all I survey"

Chapter 8 Breaking Camp

As much as I loathe the subject of the end of any trip, I must address it because it is a major part of the overall theme of a comfortable camping trip. If you've arrived home exhausted from what was supposed to be a relaxing getaway, then obviously some thing is wrong. Actually, the first place to start on planning your outings' end is to leave your home immaculate. A load or two of dirty laundry, and a bucket full of dirty camping dishes from the trip won't be so overwhelming.

When initially setting up camp, put the stuff bags for all of the tents, chairs, sleeping bags, and sleeping pads in one place perhaps in a single stuff bag which can double as a pillow. It's really frustrating trying to pack the morning of departure when nobody seems to know where they put the stuff bags. On longer trips, I start breaking down the shades on the evening before departure. Any equipment not being used beyond the last evening should be packed and ready to go. Spreading out the workload helps from becoming inundated the next morning.

Packing for departure is much easier than packing for the trip. There is no firewood to take, coolers are empty (and can serve as containers for wet or dirty laundry), and fewer provisions in general. There should be much more leg room in the back seat on the way home.

The first chore after rising for the morning is getting your sleeping pads, sleeping bags, and the underside of your tents dry. Placing the gear over a boulder in direct sunlight while you're having breakfast should be time enough to dry everything out. You don't want to pack moist sleeping pads or bags, and you're probably not going to care much for that warm musty odor when it comes time to set up camp on your next trip.

The next, and most important task, is to work on is putting the campfire completely out. Use as much water as it takes until you can put your hand into the ash without burning it. Adding a little sand (not soil, as soil may contain flammable organic material) to cover the ash surface acts as additional insurance. Cover with rocks as an added precaution.

The rest is easy; after finishing packing, "police the area". This is an old term used when I was in the Scouts to fan out and pick up (and pack out) all trash, including any discards from previous visitors. The modern term is "Leave no Trace", and means exactly what it says. Your campsite should be as left as you found it, preferably better as though you were never there. Fill in all creases, place all rocks (except those used for the fire ring) back to their original locations, and put back any natural ground cover (except that which was cleared for the fire ring) which may have been displaced.

Tip: Even though the collapsible shade arrives out of the box new with the tarp and frame packaged separately, collapse the shade leaving the tarp secured to the frame. The collapsed shade will still easily fit in the carrying case and the tarp will not be damaged. In fact, leaving the tarp secured to the frame during storage insures it will not get lost, and there is less chance the tarp will get damaged.

Cleaning Your Equipment

Most of your equipment such as camp chairs, tables, and storage bins can be cleaned like any other household item. However, tents, sleeping bags, and sleeping pads require extra special attention as you'll see.

Tents

Follow all cleaning instructions included with your tent. Tents accumulate dirt which will eventually weaken the fiber the tent is made of. Never use abrasive cleaners or solvents as they may damage the water resistant properties of your tent. I recommend cleaning your tent after every trip. If there are no specific instructions for cleaning, use warm soapy water (dishwashing liquid works great) and a sponge to wipe down the sides and floor (inside and outside). I don't recommend washing a tent in a washing machine; you'll likely destroy the tent and damage the washing machine. Before packing your tent for storage, make sure the tent is completely dry. Roll as loosely as you can to allow the tent to breath and still fit in the oversized stuff bag you bought for it. Store your tent in a cool dry place to prevent mold and mildew. I recommend applying waterproof sealant along all of the seams and spraying all zippers with a silicon lubricant before storing your tent during the off-season.

Sleeping Bags

Sleeping bags need only be cleaned when necessary, or perhaps once at the end of every season. Follow the instructions included with the sleeping bag, and check the tag usually sewn at the bottom of the bag for washing guidelines. Otherwise, for polyester sleeping bags, wash in a washing machine with a mild detergent and use a cycle for delicate apparel. You can also wash your sleeping bag by hand in the bath tub. I recommend completely unzipping the bag and turning it inside out.

If the bag is designed such that it unzips only halfway, turn the bag inside out for washing. I recommend an extra rinse cycle followed by drip drying, then perhaps a few minutes in the clothes dryer set for delicate apparel. Sleeping bags must be absolutely dry before storing to prevent mold and mildew. Rather than roll or fold the sleeping bag, stuff the sleeping bag as loosely as possible into the stuff bag to allow for breathing. Store your sleeping bags in a cool dry place.

Note: For more expensive sleeping bags, such as down filled bags, be sure to read the instructions. Even if the instructions recommend dry cleaning, never dry clean a sleeping bag, especially down filled bags. The solvents used in the dry cleaning process will remove the natural substances largely responsible for the isolative properties of the bag. I recommend hand washing down filled bags with no more than a tablespoon of mild detergent.

Sleeping Pads

If you purchased your sleeping pad, follow the instructions included with your sleeping pad; otherwise use no more than soapy water and a sponge. Similar to cleaning your tent, be sure to rinse with a damp cloth after using any cleaning agent and let the pad dry thoroughly. I use a whisk broom to clean off my foam pads from time to time, but since I just recycle these from old couches or mattresses I just throw them away after a season or two and get replacements. Using a liquid cleaner on foam will cause the foam to disintegrate and mildew. Store you sleeping pads in a cool dry place.

The Art of Tent Camping, Summary

Well, it's been fun! I've thoroughly enjoyed putting this guide together, and I hope it helps you enjoy the camping experience along with your family and friends.

Going low-tech can be a wonderful outlet for the complex and stressful lifestyles in these modern times. For me, camping is therapy and I must have this therapy as often as possible. I realize even greater rewards every time I can pass along my experiences to another generation, and that may well be my legacy. But, even though I've been on hundreds of outings, camping will always be challenging, which in turn makes every outing a unique experience. The old saying "I learn something everyday" certainly applies.

As I have mentioned, the key to a successful camping trip is to provide comfort for everyone involved at all times, and doing so in the easiest, simplest, and safest possible way. Leaving behind all of the comforts of home, and all of the technology, won't be easy at first. When I began taking the kids on my outings, I allowed cell phones (even though I knew we would be well out of range most of the time), small electronic games, music players, portable DVD players, and even Teddy Bear. I borrowed from what I learned a long time ago: if you make a big deal about something, then whatever you're making a big deal out of becomes an almost impossible situation in which to prevail (telling your daughter how much you despise her new boyfriend is just going to make her love him that much more!).

Then something amazing happened after about one camping season or so. The electronic games and DVD players were left at home by the kids' choice. Texting wasn't so important anymore. The music still went, but even that was reserved for the trip to and from our destination. An interest in the basics trumped high technology. Board games, Dominoes, and card games replaced electronic games. An afternoon of Bocce Ball, Badminton, and Horse Shoes are more fun than the mall. Staying up late to learn a few constellations, discussing the possibility of extraterrestrials, and how many stars are in our galaxy around the campfire took priority over watching a movie on a portable DVD in the tent. And it was finally decided our outings were far too dangerous for Teddy Bear, so he too was be left behind.

Chapter 9 Fishing

There are many excellent reference guides on the subject of fishing. Most guides I have reviewed get pretty technical and if you want to duplicate the authors' technique, you will probably end up spending a small fortune on rods, reels, and tackle. Most of my angling experience is river and stream fishing for both native and stocked trout in the Sierra Nevada Mountains of California and other areas in the Northwest. Since my theme for camping is simplicity, I will offer some tips on fishing while staying within the scope of my theme and use my specific experience as a point of reference for my discussion on fishing in general.

The most important topic with regards to fishing is obeying the law. Buy a fishing license and obtain a copy of rules and regulations from your states' department of fish and game. Be sure to read the rules and regulations carefully. For example, in California you can get cited for not wearing your fishing license in plain view (I'm guessing since the licenses are issued in a different color each year, this allows the warden to simply scan a river bank or lake shore using binoculars instead of having to personally hike out and check for compliance). I place my license in a plastic holder (like the kind you might see used as a visitor's pass) and safety pin it to the back of my hat. Aside from the obvious rules like limits on the number of fish you can catch per day, there may be rules on the types of hooks and bait which are allowed and the number or fishing rods allowed to be in your possession. Certain areas in California's Sierra Nevada Mountains prohibit barbed hooks. Not complying with the law can result in very stiff fines.

Before you rush out and buy a bunch of fishing poles, tackle, and bait, research the lake or river you plan to fish. Using the Internet to search by the specific name of the river or lake is a good place to start. The rivers and lakes I am accustomed to fishing are smaller by most folks' standards, and the fish (trout) range from 1 to 5 pounds. Trout are well known to be excellent fighting fish and even the stocked trout can be challenging.

I use "ultra-light" tackle, which means a small spinning reel (about 1 ½ inches in diameter), 2 pound test fishing line, and smaller split shot. I always have on hand at least 3 or 4 sizes of hooks, all small enough to completely cover with whatever bait I decide to use.

Reading the Water, and Bait

I recommend visiting the local general store nearest your destination to buy bait. The folks running the store should be happy to assist you with the best choices. They're going to know what the fish are biting and what they are not. After all, they want you to come back and buy more bait and other items as well!

Reading the water for what type of bait to use is different than reading the water as to know where to cast your line. Here, we'll talk about bait first.

Weather impacts several factors when it comes down to deciding the type of bait. If you're fishing a river, for example, a storm dozens of miles upstream can cause a normally crystal clear river to turn murky brown from all of the sediment and organic material loosened up by the storm. I would consider using night crawlers (earthworms) or crickets for bait in murky water conditions.

Clear water conditions with minimal wind means I will probably use commercial bait, and for trout fishing that usually means salmon eggs. For clear water and windy conditions, and no takers on the eggs, I might switch to a lure. By the way, it can't hurt to ask other anglers what they are using for bait. In fact, check out their stringers. Then study those anglers to see where they are casting their lines.

Reading the Water, Where are the Fish?

Finding a likely spot where fish will be hanging out isn't too difficult if you understand a few basic concepts. To begin with, you're not likely going to catch anything if the kids are throwing rocks into the lake or river. And, save the fishing until after everyone is done swimming and are out of the water.

Walk quietly as you approach or move along the shoreline. The fish can hear you. If you can see the fish, the fish can see you. Keep your shadow away from the water.

Fish need to conserve energy. For example, trout will congregate in the areas where the river current is slow. Often times that means behind rocks and closer to shore where they can scurry out into the current to catch a meal then dash back to a calm spot. In the picture shown below, I've indicated probable spots (by the dark red lines) where the water is relatively calm and where fish might likely be hanging out. Note these areas are either behind rocks, closer to shore, or behind a protrusion of shoreline caused by a bend in the river:

Trout prefer cold water. At the warmest time of the day, expect they will retreat to the deeper, shaded pools. This is one of the reasons fishing is usually better in the early mornings and later on in the evening.

If you see the stock truck pull up, don't bother rushing for your rods. Stocked trout take at least several hours to adapt to the water temperature and surrounding environment.

Ready to Cast

Since I fish the slower parts of the river, I like to cast upriver from the spot were I want the bait to settle on the bottom. Leave enough line, referred to as leader, between the hook and the split shot, about 18 inches should do. The speed of the current, and how many split shots you use, will depend on your ultimate success with hitting your target. This is where practice and skill comes in. And I can't help you with that!

Snags

You'll probably become well acquainted in a very short time with this challenging part of the fishing experience. Depending on the circumstances, you may be able to salvage your tackle even if you're snagged on the river (or lake) bottom. When I get snagged on the river bottom, I walk downstream releasing as much line as it takes to get as close to parallel between the shoreline and the snag as possible. A couple of jerks of the rod from side to side sometimes will do the trick. If you can get to the other side of the river, try jerking the rod again. The best way is to wade into the water right over the snag, and if you can't actually reach down and unhook it, try jerking the rod a couple times from side to side. Believe it or not, I've actually just waited a while to see if I get a bite or even catch a fish which obviously solves the problem. That's probably only going to happen if the split shot gets snagged as opposed to the hook getting embedded into a submerged tree branch. If you have to give up on recovering your tackle, don't stretch the line to break it. Reel in as much line as possible, then cut it.

Tackle

I quit buying rods designed to breakdown because of one experience when I cast and lost the top half of the rod. I favor a one piece rod no more than about five feet long and not too rigid. You should be able to buy this type of rod for $20.00 to $30.00 at a discount sporting goods store. But, regardless of what type of rod you prefer, take care not to slam the trunk lid or car door on the rod tip as I have done perhaps dozens of times. In fact, I include a couple of spare rod tips just in case.

I use a spinning reel as opposed to a conventional reel. Spinning reels are much easier to use while conventional reels require a little extra skill to keep the bail from spinning faster than the line is casting which causes a "rat's next", or total entanglement of most of the line in the bail. Don't bother with the cheap reels with the button like the one pictured below. They are prone to tangle and probably won't last the first fishing trip.

Fishing line is one piece of tackle I do recommend not going too cheap with. You might pay $10.00 or $12.00 for several hundred yards of a brand name roll. This is more than enough to load several small bails. If your reel comes already loaded with fishing line, consider replacing it with better quality line.

Just like the first aid kit I put together, I prefer a heavy plastic tackle box which unfolds into two or three trays. There's enough space for all your bait and tackle, but you'll want to include maybe some bandages, matches, insect repellent, head net, and anything you might need during a few hours of fishing without having to go all the way back to camp.

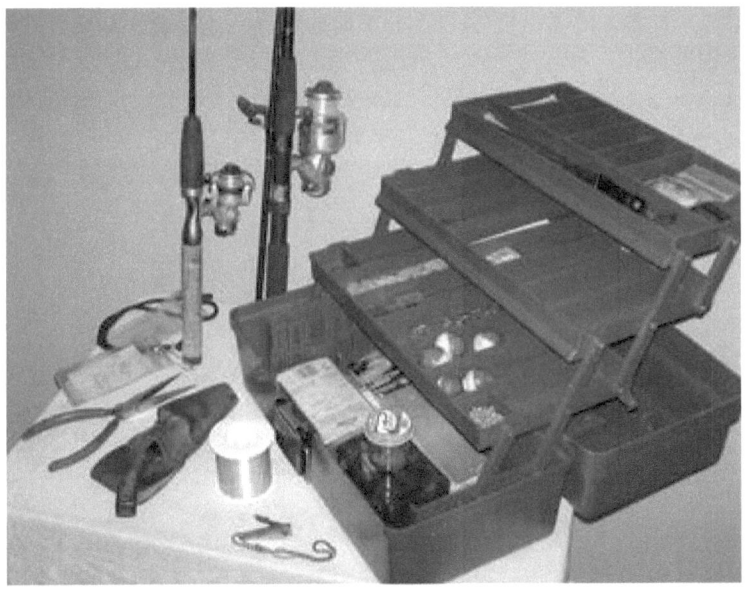

One piece of equipment I haven't discussed is the stringer. Hopefully, you will need it. There are many types of stringers such as the one that looks like a chain with clips for each fish. These are more expensive, but they are handy. I use the simple version, about four feet of nylon cordage, one end is crimped to a steel ring about an inch and a half in diameter, the other end crimped into a sharpened steel point about three inches long.

Using the clip type, you simply insert the clip into the gill and out of the mouth of the fish, then attach the clip to the chain. The principle is the same for the nylon stringer; thread the sharp end through the gill and out the mouth of the fish. Then thread the sharp end through the ring. Place the stringer with the fish in the water to keep them fresh, and tie the other end of the stringer securely to a rock or tree branch.

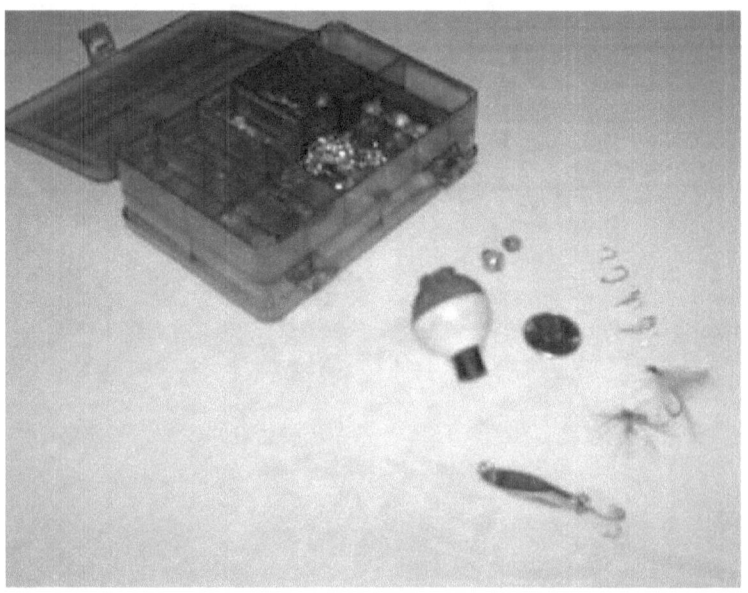

In addition to hooks, split shot, bait, and extra line, your tackle should include a fish net, needle nose pliers, and a nail clipper. I like to attach a small nail clipper to my belt using a shoelace for easy access. I find that a nail clipper is the best tool for cutting off excess line after tying off hooks or leaders. I also have a sheath I wear on my belt to carry the needle nose pliers and a small fixed blade knife.

Cleaning Your Catch

I use a 5 gallon bucket about half full of river (or lake) water to clean my catch. In this way I can dispatch the contents after I am done into hole which I have already dug well away from any campsite, fresh water source, and trail (200 to 300 feet is strongly encouraged). The river stays clean and I don't attract critters to any of the campsites in the area.

Filleting a fish is a process whereby a fillet knife is used to slice each side of the fish from where the tail begins up to just before the gills and as closely to the rib cage as possible. Smaller fish are usually not filleted because there isn't very much meat produced as a result.

I prefer to gut smaller fish such as trout. It's quick and easy once you've done it a few times and there isn't as much wasted meat. Start by slicing the underside of the fish from the poop chute all the way to the front of the lower jaw. Hold the fish using one hand while pulling all the internal organs out with your other hand. The hardest part is to detach the organs from the head; you have to pull a little harder. After all the organs have been removed, you'll notice a narrow streak of dark material directly under the spine and running the length of the spine. Using your thumb nail, gouge out all of the dark material. Rinse the fish as often as needed. Upon cleaning all of your catch, do a final rinse in clean water.

I don't find that scaling trout is necessary. I also prefer to leave the head and tail on during cooking. There are many recipes for preparing trout and other fish which can be found by searching the Internet. I prefer pan frying in butter and white wine. In my opinion, simple recipes are better because I don't want to lose the taste of the freshest fish you can get!

Fishing, Summary

I have shared with you some fundamental common sense techniques and the basic equipment necessary for a successful fishing adventure based on my personal experience. Fishing is a sport where there is always room for improvement and you're always learning something new. I compare learning the sport of fishing to walking into a gym for the first time. When I walk into that gym I'm going to look for the person who has the physique I desire, and study their workout. When fishing, it's always the angler with the most fish on their stringer who I want to study.

One piece of advice when it comes to fishing: just like I discussed back in the camping summary, beware of gadgets. You can end up spending a lot of money for bait and tackle that only works great on TV or the Internet.

Appendix A, Equipment and Provision Checklists

Even though I've been on hundreds of camping trips, just like a flight plan, I still like to have a list I can refer to. I try to avoid that "what did I forget" feeling once I've pulled out of the driveway. This is the check list I have posted on my refrigerator door, and I use it every trip. Compose one for yourself!

[ ] **"Art of Tent Camping, The"**
[ ] Axe
[ ] Bath tissue

[ ] Binoculars; **Tip:** the better quality binoculars, the happier you will be with this investment. Not only will features in daytime be far better enhanced, nighttime viewing of the skies offers a better look at the moon, planets, and even a few distant galaxies.

[ ] Boots, Shoes (water shoes)

[ ] Buckets; **Tip:** a five gallon bucket is an extremely versatile piece of equipment. They're useful for washing dishes, laundry, pre-cooling drinks, and along with a small plastic shovel, the little campers can use it down by the river for collecting crawdads or tadpoles.

[ ] Can holders, insulated
[ ] Can opener
[ ] Canteen
[ ] Chairs
[ ] Coffee pot, filters
[ ] Cooking utensils, pots, pans
[ ] Coolers
[ ] Cork screw

[ ] Dish soap, sponge
[ ] Duct tape
[ ] Fire extinguisher
[ ] Firewood
[ ] Flashlights, extra batteries

[ ] Games: Badminton, Board Games, Bocce Balls, Frisbee, Glow Sticks, Horse Shoes, Kite, Playing Cards

[ ] Gloves
[ ] Hats
[ ] Hot dog sticks
[ ] Insect repellant
[ ] Insect traps
[ ] Knife
[ ] Lady Campers – That Time of the Month
[ ] Lantern
[ ] Lighter fluid

[ ] Maps; **Tip:** Use transparent plastic contact sheeting to laminate paper maps. This protects the maps from the elements and they last longer.

[ ] Matches; **Tip:** take wood stick matches and waterproof by submerging the tip of the match in melted candle wax. I have matches I waterproofed some forty years ago, and they still work!

[ ] Mosquito netting
[ ] Multi-Tool

[ ] Pillows, blankets (optional, but consider for the ride to and from your destination)

[ ] Plastic bags (Trash, Freezer Storage Bags, etc)
[ ] Ponchos, Rain Suits
[ ] Propane

[ ] Napkins (I prefer napkins over paper towels because they are much less expensive)

[ ] Paper plates, cups
[ ] Portable potty
[ ] Radio, portable AM, 2 way
[ ] Rake
[ ] Rope, 50 feet ¼ inch, and 100 feet 3/8 inch
[ ] Scarves
[ ] Shade
[ ] Shovel
[ ] Sleeping bags
[ ] Sleeping pads
[ ] Stove
[ ] Sun glasses, strap
[ ] Sun screen
[ ] Tents, poles, stakes, rain flies
[ ] Tool box
[ ] Toothbrushes, toothpaste, floss
[ ] Umbrella, stand
[ ] Water jug (5 to 6 gallons, full)

[ ] Water Sports: Floating Lounges, Inner Tubes, Personal Floatation Devices (PFD's), Pump, Water Shoes

Appendix B, Last Minute Items, Night Before Departure Checklist

[ ] Cash, a couple of blank checks (a check could come in handy for paying camping use fees)

[ ] Extra vehicle key, store somewhere outside the vehicle, perhaps with the camping kitchen equipment. I definitely do not recommend one of those magnetic hide-a-key gadgets. I've lost every one I've tried.

[ ] Food, dry perishable, including bread, coffee
[ ] Food, frozen, hot dogs
[ ] Food, refrigerated, including milk, condiments
[ ] Gas up vehicle

Last Minute List, Morning of Departure Checklist

[ ] Cell phone, charger
[ ] Ice up coolers
[ ] Prescription medications
[ ] Reading and sun glasses
[ ] Thermos with coffee (I make mine the night before)

Appendix C, First Aid Kit Checklist

[ ] Alcohol swabs
[ ] Baby powder

[ ] Bandages, recommend 3 inch by ¾ inch, you can always trim them down.

[ ] Cloth surgical tape, 2 inches by 10 yards.
[ ] Cotton swabs
[ ] Elastic bandage, 3 or 4 inches by 10 yards

[ ] Gauze, sterile, twenty 4 inch by 4 inch pads, and a couple rolls of 3 inch by 10 yards.

[ ] Hydrogen Peroxide, 8 ounce bottle

[ ] Antacid
[ ] Antibiotic ointment
[ ] Antiseptic

[ ] Cold and cough medication in both adult and little camper strengths

[ ] Hydrocortisone
[ ] Ipecac syrup*
[ ] Menthol rub

[ ] Candle
[ ] Eye wash cup**
[ ] Lantern mantles
[ ] Hand lotion
[ ] Hand soap
[ ] Nail clippers
[ ] Oral thermometer (non-mercury/non-glass)
[ ] Safety pins

[ ] Sewing, button kit

[ ] Shampoo, conditioner (I save those small containers provided by hotels)

[ ] Shoe and boot laces
[ ] Surgical scissors
[ ] Tweezers, one each small and large size

* Ipecac syrup is used to induce vomiting in certain emergency situations. Only certified medical personnel should be consulted regarding appropriate use of Ipecac syrup.

** The eyewash cup is a small plastic, oval shaped cup which fits over the eye socket. I have used it for removing small debris from underneath the eyelid. Fill with distilled water and placed over the eye, then blink to remove the debris. This simple little gadget can save your whole trip.

Appendix D, Knots and Tie Downs

There are three basic knots I use frequently. These knots are easy to learn to tie and will work for any situation requiring the securing of rope or cordage

Taunt Line

The Taunt Line (also known as three "half hitches") may be used to tie down everything from the heaviest loads (for example, appliances), or the guy lines on my camping shower. Just like a load shifts on a moving vehicle, the guy lines on camping equipment also shift as a result of wind, soft ground, or me tripping over them. It only takes a few seconds to tighten them all up. Another added bonus is unlike spaghetti knots, half-hitches are easy to untie allowing the cordage to be reused.

In the picture above, I have strung the rope through a hard point followed by making two loops on the inside of the knot (towards the hard point). Take the end and string it towards the outside of the knot and make the final loop. Tighten the knot and you will now be able to slide the knot up the rope to secure your load.

Square Knot

The Square Knot is another simple knot primarily useful for tying smaller lengths of rope together to make a longer length of rope. Tied correctly, the Square Knot will not slip or untie due to stress from securing even the heaviest of loads. And the Square Knot is easy to untie allowing the cordage to be reused.

Tying a square knot is similar to double tying your shoe laces. Loop the rope end held in your left hand over the rope end held in your right hand. So far, you have tied half the knot. Loop the end of the rope which originated in your left hand over the end of the rope which originated in your right hand. Tighten the knot by pulling each length of rope.

Bowline

Mountaineers and rock climbers depend on this knot with their lives. Unlike the Taunt Line which may need to be tightened periodically due to stress, the Bowline will not slip. The Bowline is used primarily to tie of one end of a rope to a hard point such as a tree while the other end might be secured to tent poles using the Taunt Line as an additional anchor against high wind.

Loop the rope around the hard point you wish to tie off to using the Bowline knot. In the example above I am demonstrating how the Bowline is effective to tie myself off. In this example, I loop a section of rope around my left hand. Keeping the loop rigid, I pull a section of rope though the loop creating another loop. The other end of the rope (painted orange) is strung through the loop which I had just pulled through the first loop.

The picture above shows that pulling on the rope away from the Bowline tightens the knot. The Bowline knot will easily accommodate your own weight and potentially even more, assuming the cordage is rated appropriately.

Tie Downs

Tie downs are straps which have a variety of mechanisms by which to tighten down a load, for example, to your roof rack or the contents in the bed of a pickup truck. I prefer two types of tie downs; one type which has a buckle or spring loaded "jaw" for gripping the strap as it's being tightened down, the other has a winch on one end for tightening the strap. Both straps have an "S" hook on the other end for easy attachment to a hard point. Both of these types of straps are easy to use to secure and unsecure cargo. I recommend straps which are rated at perhaps a quarter or half ton, if not more.

Shown above is one end of a tie down with an "S" hook on one end secured to a hard point.

Shown above is a buckle, or spring loaded jaw type tie down. The jaw is easier to use but I don't recommend it for heavy loads.

Shown below is the ratchet type tie down. Securing a load is much easier and the ratchet will easily handle heavy loads. The ratchet type tie down, however, is difficult to release because two hands (and sometimes three) are necessary to pull multiple release mechanisms.

Appendix E, More Camping Accessories

Portable Fan

Fortunately before one of my warm (actually hot) weather trips, I bought a small portable fan. Nothing fancy, just a two speed fan that uses two D cell batteries. If you have ever spent the night when the temperature doesn't drop below eighty degrees until an hour or so *before* sun up, then you know how miserable it is trying to get some sleep. An alternative to beating the heat is to sleep out under the stars on the beach next to the river or lake. But the rules of the campground usually don't permit camping of any kind near a fresh water source.

The fan cost about $7.00 at a well known big box store. I put brand new batteries in the fan and it lasted all night every night for six nights. This is a cheap version of more expensive fans (which I intend to upgrade to), but I wanted to try out the concept before investing in anything more expensive. One problem I noticed was after I installed the batteries to test it before leaving on my trip was the sliding power switch located on one side of the fan. I had to tape the switch in the off position so the switch wouldn't accidentally move to the on position while packing it back in the box. Otherwise, the fan was a complete success!

Another useful accessory I found useful at a garage sale for a buck is an old analog thermometer. It has three needles, one for lowest recorded temperature, one for highest recorded temperature, and of course one for current temperature.

I just leave it out all week and monitor it when I get up in the morning. I also like to know what the low temperatures are especially during cold weather camping. This helps me assess my equipment. I haven't looked, but there must be digital versions available too. I doubt this old piece is still made but it works great and doesn't need batteries. Simple yet elegant!

Cooking Using a Spit over an Open Campfire

I had originally come up with idea of building my own spit using steel rods for the posts and a stainless steel rod as the spit. I spent a fair amount of time chasing down the materials with little success. And after trying to find an establishment to weld my design per my specifications, I gave up because it was going to be too expensive and for whatever reason, I was unable to communicate to the gentlemen doing the welding exactly what I wanted as the end result. I decided to search the Internet (which is what I should have done in the first place) and found exactly what I wanted:

Instead of two posts, there is only one post which is obviously easier to set up (note the post is set just outside the campfire ring). The carriage in which the spit is inserted slides from the top of the post and is easily adjustable, up and down, and left and right. The battery pack containing two "D" sized batteries snaps to the rear of the carriage and turns the spit at perhaps twenty revolutions per minute. In addition to adjusting the spit, you can use your shovel to move coals allowing complete control of the heat.

Note: never cook over a campfire using treated wood. Treated wood contains harmful chemicals.

The concept is to slow cook whatever you skewer. Allow more time for larger birds and roasts and count on starting the campfire right after lunch to obtain a good sized bed of hot coals to cook over. Plan on the rest of the day before the roast is done. Pictured above are a couple of game hens, about 3 pounds each. They took about three hours to cook all the way through. Baste with garlic butter and sage, and it is well worth the time and effort! Improvise by attaching a basket and slow roast shrimp, fish, and smaller game birds.

I don't use my spit in hotter months where standing around a campfire is too uncomfortable. But it's perfect for cold weather camping if you want to stay warm and have a great dinner!

This spit design is compact, reasonably lightweight, easy to setup, breakdown, clean, store, and packs nicely along with other camping gear. A new set of batteries will last several uses.

Cooking Using a Grill over an Open Campfire

Another adaptation of the concept of cooking over an open fire using one post set just outside of the campfire ring uses a grill. The grill slides over the post, is adjustable for height, and swivels to either side. Again, this allows for greater control over how much heat is desired for whatever food is to be cooked on the grill:

Shown above is the grill featuring a cooking sheet for foods such as smaller seafood, fish fillets, and vegetables which might otherwise fall through the grill. By the way, if the kids aren't too keen on the veggies, try grilling squash, eggplant, or bacon wrapped asparagus. You may be pleasantly surprised how quickly the veggies vanish!

This grill design is easy to setup, breakdown, store, and packs nicely along with other camping gear. But, like any other grills, it's a bit challenging to clean.

Index